Emma Gomez:

A Courageous Woman Displays True Grit

Emma Gomez

iUniverse LLC
Bloomington

EMMA GOMEZ: A COURAGEOUS WOMAN DISPLAYS TRUE GRIT

iUniverse books may be ordered through booksellers or by contacting:

iUniverse LLC
1663 Liberty Drive
Bloomington, IN 47403
www.iuniverse.com
1-800-Authors (1-800-288-4677)

Because of the dynamic nature of the Internet, any web addresses or links contained in this book may have changed since publication and may no longer be valid. The views expressed in this work are solely those of the author and do not necessarily reflect the views of the publisher, and the publisher hereby disclaims any responsibility for them.

Any people depicted in stock imagery provided by Thinkstock are models, and such images are being used for illustrative purposes only.
Certain stock imagery © Thinkstock.

ISBN: 978-1-4917-3647-0 (sc)
ISBN: 978-1-4917-3648-7 (e)

Library of Congress Control Number: 2014910325

Printed in the United States of America.

iUniverse rev. date: 06/13/2014

To Professor Pablo Ortiz-Cotto, who guided me along the road to success. Pablo, I miss you and I wish you were here to enjoy the end results and to be proud of me one more time. I will always remember you. I also dedicate this book to my one and only grandson, Gavin, whom I love dearly. He is my angel and my reason for living. Nana will always love you, angel.

CONTENTS

PREFACE

Professor Barbara Wertheimer developed the idea for this book to be written in 1976, during my second year in college when I was in my early forties. At that time she was one of my instructors and also my counselor. Barbara and I used to meet often for brief conversations. One day when we met, she mentioned the idea of my writing a book. I thought she was kidding when she said, "Emma, I think you should write a book." She understood my surprise and said, "Think about it." Nothing further was said about the topic that day.

The next time we met, she again mentioned that I write a book. I asked her what made her think I could write a book and what would it be about. Her response was quick and simple: "I have been watching you, and you have the potential." She was aware of the fact that I was involved in the labor movement. In her own words, she felt that I had a "commendable ability to deal with labor issues affecting workingwomen." I told her I didn't even know how to start. The last thing that Barbara told me was, "Try to make an outline of what you want to say." I never saw her again. Unknown to me, Barbara had been suffering from lung cancer; she passed away at age fifty-two.

Her idea of my writing a book faded away. But I continued with my studies and my activities. As time went by, some friends and other people around me often suggested that I should write a book about my life experiences and achievements. They believed my life story could help its readers to improve their quality of life. So, over three decades later, Barbara's idea of writing a book about my life became reality.

Acknowledgments

I sincerely thank my daughter, Emmaline, and her husband, Aaron, for their professional help preparing documents and illustrations for the printing of my book.

I also thank the friendly and caring team of doctors who are helping me remain in good health: Dr. Wagdy Girgis, my family doctor; his assistant, Dr. Irina Busnic; and Dr. Anthony Maniscalco, my neurologist. They are commendable health-care providers, and I appreciate their professional service and their sense of humor.

I thank Samantha Gladd for installing the Microsoft Word program for me.

I also thank my son, Peter, for driving me anywhere I needed to go for book materials.

INTRODUCTION

This book is an effort to invite readers to learn about the actions, events, and perhaps unique experiences of my life. I consider some of these childhood experiences—especially those in a rural community during the late thirties and early forties—to be unique because of the time and place in which they occurred. It was the time when families were experiencing the devastation of the Second World War.

The book is a genuine reflection of my life. The stories, decisions, and actions mentioned throughout this book are my own. My name is Emma, and I was born in Puerto Rico in 1934 and raised in the mountains of the small town of Yabucoa. This picturesque town is on the southeast coast of the island. One of the main reasons I wrote this book was to share my experiences with readers so they can keep them in mind in case they are faced with similar situations in their own lives. It could be like taking a journey to the past and then coming back to the present with a better understanding of yourself and those around you.

My Childhood

My parents were two remarkable human beings, who lived in the mountains almost their entire lives. My father, Narciso Rodriguez, was a farmer with a fourth-grade education. My mother, Dolores Surillo, was a housewife and never went to school. But regardless of their limited education, they raised their ten children, who attended school and grew up being respected and responsible citizens. For my parents, education was a priority that could not be compromised in any way. All ten children were born at home with help from a midwife.

When I talk about my childhood, it brings back memories that could be hard for others to believe. Imagine a child without a toy, without shoes, and sleeping on an improvised bed. I had only a few pieces of homemade clothing, for my parents could not provide anything else. At night, our home was under the light of a candle because electricity service had not reached our rural community yet. Mother tried her best to make her children comfortable, and despite our difficult situation, we were happy and in good health. Although our situation might seem unimaginable for today's generation, back then it was reality. You didn't miss what you never had or didn't know existed.

Regardless of the lack of everyday necessities, Mother made sure we were not hungry, were clean, and slept well. As unendurable as it might seem, I can say my childhood was good. I had a mother who cared for her children, provided them the main necessities, and kept them away from danger the best she could.

As I grew up, Mother did what every mother should do: she instilled in me, among other things, respect and the sense of responsibility. Mother set me up in the right direction to a meaningful and productive future.

Today, in my senior years, I still live in New York City, where I have been living since I left the mountains of Yabucoa. Although I am not rich, I am living a happy and comfortable life with the support of the relatives near me: my son, Peter, and his wife, Sonia; my sister, Benedicta; and my husband, Freddy. My daughter, Emmaline, is not near me, but I have her support as well as that of Aaron, her husband. I still practice what I learned in my childhood, which is to accept responsibility for my actions regardless of their nature and to respect the actions of others regardless of who they are or where they come from. My children and other relatives live by the same principles.

When writing about my life, I do not consider any statistics. I base my writing on what I have observed and learned from others, and on my own life experiences.

GROWING UP IN THE MOUNTAINS OF YABUCOA

Growing up in the mountains was an experience that I call an adventure. Mountains are nature at its best. Those of us who have lived in or have visited the mountains almost always have interesting stories to tell. Some of my stories are humorous, some are hard to believe, and others are both of the above. It was a time in my life that I will never forget. Living in the mountains and lacking necessities was not a sign of poverty. It was just a sign of the times; we could not have what was not available to us. That was the way it was for my family in the thirties.

I will tell readers some of the stories that I best recall. I will also tell them about some events and activities unique to life in an undeveloped rural community, as mine was. I say unique because there was no choice. We had to accept whatever was in front of us or have nothing. Residents of a community without paved roads, without means of communication, and with no means of transportation but walking knew they were on their own. They had to provide their families the daily necessities using their own means and methods. My parents did just that. I believe this is unique of an undeveloped community because of the fact that residents knew they had no choice; if they didn't do it, they just had to do without it—whatever it was they were looking for.

Here is one of my humorous and hard-to-believe stories. My parents did not allow any of their young children to go out after dark. But one evening, Guillito, a young family friend, asked Father to let Margaret and I go with him to a party at a neighbor's house. Father looked at Guillito and said, "I will let them go as long as you bring them back to me safe and sound." And to the party we went. Margaret was fourteen and I was seventeen years old. Tito, a boy who was not well liked by the community, asked Margaret to dance with him and she said no. Everybody was having fun until Margaret went to dance with another boy. Tito approached the couple and hit the fellow in the face. A fight broke out, and I pulled Margaret toward a bedroom window. We climbed on the bed and reached for the window, accidentally stepping over a young boy who was sleeping. When I pushed Margaret out the window, her skirt got caught on a bedpost and ripped. I followed her, jumping out the window and running home in the dark.

Fortunately, Father wasn't expecting us back home that early, so he was taking a nap. We were able to enter our bedroom and go to bed without waking up Father. A while later Father got up, and while walking toward the balcony, he noticed we were in bed. He also noticed Guillito waiting for him by the balcony. Guillito had no idea where we were. And lucky Guillito experienced his second shock of the night. Before he had a chance to say a word, Father thanked him for bringing his daughters back so early, adding that we were sleeping. Father and Mother never knew our story. To this day, every time Margaret and I tell the story, we just have a good laugh. As for Guillito, he felt like the luckiest man in the world.

Another unique and hard-to-believe story is as follows. Along the road to school, some residents from the community had dogs for their protection. These dogs were big and vicious. They scared almost everyone passing by. One day as I went by, a dog ran after me. I escaped its attack by running as fast as I could on an unpaved road—without shoes. I was able to escape the attack because the dog was at a short distance from the road when it barked. So I started to run before it did. Everyone thought it was funny, but for me, it was the scare of my life.

As far as I remember, until I was six or seven years old, we lived on a big property owned by Don Emiliano, a family friend. This was a large and convenient property. There was a brook with clean and clear water nearby, from which we carried water to the house for daily use. The containers used to carry the water were made by Mother using fruit from the higuera tree. This fruit resembles a pumpkin, but it is much stronger. The house was big and well kept. I don't recall what the inside of the house was made of, but it was comfortable. Some of us slept in hammocks; others, including me, slept on top of a padded wood-grain container. This is the place where I was born. I had nine siblings, two brothers and seven sisters. Following is our birth order: Nick, Juanita (now deceased), Rose, Mary, Fausto (recently deceased), Carmen, me, Margaret, Benedicta, and Sylvia.

In the late thirties, Father purchased a piece of land nearby where we were living. Soon after, with help from the family and neighbors, Father built a frame house and painted it blue. It had three bedrooms and a large living room, and we quickly moved to the blue house. I remember how happy we were living in our own house. Father kept purchasing land as it became available until the family owned eight acres, which we still own. And though we still own the property, none of us is planning on going back to it. Today the property stands alone and un-kept, except for a small part near the road being used and well kept by a neighbor.

By the early forties, sisters Juanita and Rose had left home looking for work. Brother Nick was called for military duty and was sent away to serve during the Second World War. The blue house was not as big as the previous one; but since three of the children had left home, there was ample space for the rest of us. Meanwhile, Father was planning to build a bigger and better house. So with the small amount of money received for Nick's military service, he started his project. Now that we had enough land, Father was ready to build a family home that could last forever.

With the oldest three siblings gone, Father was left with the younger ones, some too young to offer their help. He put all of us to help in the construction of the new house according to our age and ability. However, Father set time for everything and did not overwork any of us. He never compromised our daily chores, especially our schoolwork. The youngest four, including me, carried the water for daily consumption from the creek on our property to the house. Almost always, we helped Father on weekends only. We also carried water for the cement mixing needed to make the cinder blocks used for the new house.

The project lasted several years, but it didn't matter because we were enjoying the blue house. Finally the bigger and better house was completed. It was a very comfortable home, with four bedrooms, a large living room, a small area for cooking, a bathroom, and a balcony. I can't recall when the family moved from the blue house to the new house, but I believe it was in the late forties, after the war. The credit for this remarkable achievement went to everyone around: the entire family, friends, and neighbors.

The eight sisters and the two brothers never had an opportunity to all be together at any time, for when the younger ones were born, the older ones had left home in search of work to support themselves. Once gone, it was difficult for them to visit the rest of the family on their own. Since there were no jobs available in the small cities nearby, they traveled far away to the big cities to find some maintenance work or anything else available.

With the older ones gone and construction of the new house completed, the rest of us had some time to play our favorite games. Some young relatives and friends living nearby came over to play with us around the house. We played games such as jumping rope, jumping squares, hide-and-seek, and others. My parents enjoyed watching us play, especially in the evenings after school. Those were some unforgettable moments of my life. It was also a time when most children were respectful and well behaved. And here is a happy note: the concrete structure of the new house is still standing. As Father once said: "Forever."

Time went by. Brother Nick and Sister Mary got married and left home. Then Brother Fausto left home for New York. Sister Carmen got married and also left home. Soon after graduating from high school, I left for New York also. Several years went by before I was able to visit my parents due to my own commitments.

My Parents

To raise ten children is a complex and challenging endeavor. It is a difficult-to-handle task for anyone at any time, but this is especially true for people with limited resources and hardly any education. My parents did it with hard work, with pride, and with dignity. For my parents, education was a priority that could not be compromised in any way.

Mother made sure our homework was done and that we went to bed early, got to school on time, and were well groomed. When the school day was over, we were to be home at a certain time or get scolded and perhaps punished. There were several things that upset Mother the most, which were disobeying her, talking back to her, and lying. Most of the time, she just scolded us; but if we did not listen, she had us washing dishes for a week. Carmen was the only one who gave Mother a hard time. I never experienced any scolding or punishment, but some of my sisters say they did. In the farm or in the house, we had no problem complying with our duties as assigned. In the house we washed dishes, but our main responsibility was to carry the water for daily consumption from the brook to the house before going to school.

Mother's house chores were endless, but somehow she always managed to stay in control. Father was responsible for the farm, its products, and the farm animals. The cow produced milk for the family, and the horse was for Father's transportation. Mother took care of the chickens and their eggs, which were sold for cash to purchase those necessities the farm could not produce.

My parents had opposite personalities. Mother was a strong disciplinarian who kept to herself. She seldom smiled and never told jokes. Father was more of a joker, with a great sense of humor. Working with him on the farm was easy. He seemed relaxed, even when he wasn't. He loved to make people laugh. This is one of his stories, which after decades, still makes us laugh. When moving to the blue house, the first things he moved were his little girls: baby Sylvia, Benedicta, Margaret, and me. Being the oldest of the four, I looked after the other three while Father went for more stuff to bring to the blue house. It was raining hard, and the dirt road was flooded with clay mud. And there was a steep cliff on one side of the road. Father was carrying our dinner and he fell in the mud. When he got to us, he said, "Before you eat your dinner, check it out; it might have some mud in it. I fell in the mud and some of the mud got inside the dinner containers. I cleaned it off, but check it out anyway before you eat it." We did as he said, but it seemed fine to us. So we ate it, and then we had a good laugh. Everything Father did had some humor in it. His view of life was always positive. His sense of humor made him likable and respected.

One of Father's main farm products was tobacco. Although some laborers complained about the product being sticky and smelly, Father had no problems with it. He taught family members what to do and how to do it to prepare the product for the market. In his humorous way, he said this to us: "I am going to show you how to stick the needle in the tobacco leaves, and not in your fingers." He was talking about the first stage the leaves had to go through before being market ready. We were to put two leaves back to back and stick the needle with the string through the center of the two leaves. We then continued the process, making a garland-like string of leaves to be hung to dry.

I strongly believe that parents are the best role models for their children. Naturally, children like to follow what they see; therefore, it is up to the parents to set the pattern for their children to follow. Today, I am proud of my parents for teaching us well.

SIBLINGS

As I said above, the eight sisters and the two brothers never had an opportunity to be all together at any time, because when the younger ones were born, the older ones had already left home in search of work to support themselves. The separation from her children caused Mother some emotional stress, but since there was no choice, she gave us her blessing. This made it easier and less physically stressful for her to care for the younger ones.

The lessons we learned from Mother during our childhood helped us to find work. We were willing and able to accept any kind of work offered to us. We were well spoken and respectful, and although our attire was modest, we gave a good physical appearance.

Early in life, we learned to understand that our parents could not offer us any more than what they already had offered. It was up to us to look for new horizons, and we did it successfully. Our parents knew without a doubt that we would do well because they had taught us well. As adults, we would subconsciously practice what we learned during our childhood.

I believe what we learn during childhood stays with us for the rest of our lives. Unfortunately, today some parents are seemingly not aware of how important childhood is in their children's development. They fail to prepare the children for the challenges and inequalities they will encounter in our society today.

Discipline must begin at home while children are just starting to learn and to understand the new world around them. If parents do not discipline their children at home, there might be problems with the child's behavior as he or she grows up. My parents knew that teaching good manners and good behavior was not the teacher's responsibility, but their own. With limited knowledge in these essential factors, my parents did the best they could to prepare all of us for both our near future and the one beyond.

My conviction on the importance of raising children properly was set by my own observations of my sisters and brothers and the achievements of us all. With the exception of the three youngest sisters, the rest of us experienced difficult times while growing up. In rural areas like ours, there was no electricity, no running water, no paved roads, no transportation, and no facilities of any kind nearby. But amid all these drawbacks, we became well educated and respected human beings. For example: after his military service during the Second World War, Nick, my oldest brother, went back to school and earned his PhD in education, and then served as a professor at the University of Puerto Rico. My sister Margaret, after raising her three children and mastering the English language, went back to school and earned a master's degree, also in education. Then she served as a teacher in the New York City public schools.

My brother Fausto (now deceased), with just a fourth-grade education, also learned the English language and became a businessman. After working in a fast-food restaurant and saving money, he purchased a grocery store and enjoyed great success. He was able to put his two sons through college and to purchase their own home. After raising my two children, I went back to school in my mid-forties and earned a bachelor's degree in labor and management. Then I was promoted to a building manager specialist position in the federal service. My sister Benedicta went back to school and graduated as a registered nurse.

My sister Sylvia served in the US Air Force for four years in several locations, including two years in the US embassy in Bolivia, South America. The four oldest sisters—Juanita (deceased), Rose, Mary, and Carmen—did not go back to school. However, they successfully raised their children and made their own money at home by sewing—except Rose, who worked as a supervisor in a perfume factory.

People say we were lucky, but our success was not due to luck. It was because of our parent's hard work while raising us. My parents knew they were responsible for all of us siblings, with no other resources but their hard work. And they never experienced any regret. My family is a good example of how the lessons learned during childhood are evidently displayed during adulthood.

SCHOOL YEARS

For most children the first year in school is an unforgettable experience, and mine was too. To this day, I can't tell with certainty the year, and my age, when I started first grade. It should be easy to figure it out considering the standard six years of age when starting first grade, plus twelve school years to complete high school. I should have been eighteen years old after finishing high school. But I was not. I attended school for eleven years because I skipped one year, so I should have been seventeen years old after completing high school. But I wasn't. I graduated from high school in 1953, at nineteen years of age. And that is what I know accurately.

While I was in first grade, my parents knew what to expect from me. They knew I had the potential to be an excellent student, and I did not disappoint them. Ironically, Cruz Sanchez, my teacher, was a woman with a personality similar to my mother's. She was a no-nonsense person who meant what she said. Right from the beginning, she explained to us what she expected from us. We were to pay attention to her, learn our lessons, and behave. If we did not, she was ready to use "the ruler" on us. With her wooden ruler, she would hit those students who were not listening to her or were misbehaving. To make us listen and learn, she would hit the student a few times on the legs. At that time, teachers were allowed to punish children, cautiously, whenever necessary. Though she was known as one of the best teachers, some students were afraid of her. Only a few of her students escaped the ruler. I was one of them.

Regardless of her teaching methods, Ms. Sanchez was our teacher for three consecutive years. By the end of the third grade, students liked her and respected her more than they had during previous years. Parents were grateful to her for teaching their children well. Her students did so well that some were skipped to higher grades. I skipped from the fourth grade to the sixth grade. I have no recollection of what my schoolbooks looked like during my primary and secondary school years—perhaps because at the time, all textbooks in Puerto Rico were in English, and some students had problems understanding the material. The reason for this was that at that time, Puerto Rico was not a commonwealth, as it is now. The commonwealth system of government gave residents the right to elect their own governor and to declare Spanish their main language. For me, doing my schoolwork was easy, but getting to the classroom was not. As I mentioned earlier, I had no shoes during my first school years. And the school was several miles away from my home. There was no transportation to and from school other than walking.

I should mention to readers that a classroom approximately sixty-five years ago can't be compared with today's classroom. It would be hard for readers to believe such a classroom even if they were able to see it. It is just unimaginable for today's students. However, students years ago were satisfied with what they had because they knew that besides the basics—blackboards, chalk, erasers, and pencils—nothing else was available for them. Nevertheless, I must say that school was not always work and no fun. We had days on which students could demonstrate their talents, such as storytelling, and other talents like mine: I enjoyed reciting poems. This is my favorite memory of my early school years.

To complicate the matter, the road was unpaved, and some residents of the community had vicious dogs for their personal protection. Though not often, these dogs attacked the passersby, making the trip to school a real challenge. We had to be prepared to run for safety every time we went by. One day, a dog ran after me, and I escaped the attack by running as fast as I could, without shoes on an unpaved road. I must tell you, it was not fun. The only reason I was able to escape the attack was because the dog was a short distance from the road when it barked, so I started to run way before it did.

Amid these incredible stories, I graduated from the first grade with the highest marks, and from the sixth grade with the second highest. But my struggles continued and became more complex and daring than the previous ones. Only one thing made a difference: I had shoes. Soon, another difficult situation was about to begin for me. The junior high school was much farther from home than the previous school; thank heaven I had shoes. This time I was walking over four miles each way. Though the road was partially paved, it was still a difficult situation. There was a small part of the road that was almost impossible to pass. It was a steep hill, with rocks and boulders that had crevices and holes everywhere and nothing to hold onto. The only way to avoid this dangerous hill was to go through an adjacent private property full of trees, large bushes, and all kinds of insects and creatures ready to bite you.

On the paved section of the road, there was a more serious problem. Endless sugarcane plantations lined the road all the way to the end of the road. Because of their thickness and wildness, these plantations became homes for criminals, making it easy for them to attack their victims. To worsen the already dangerous conditions, at one time an armed prisoner escaped from prison, and according to the authorities, he was hiding in the sugarcane plantations. His name was Correa Cotto, and he had a criminal history that made headlines throughout the island of Puerto Rico. This incident was the talk of the town. Everywhere you went, people knew about it. Others were reading newspapers or listening to the radio. Needless to say, my parents were very concerned and worried. Father made sure he remained informed, either by reading the newspaper or listening to our battery-powered radio.

I never saw anything or anyone suspicious, but I was concerned and afraid. I always tried not walking alone, but at times I had to. I never took for granted anything moving or any noise. I was always alert and walking fast. I even thought that, since I had run faster than a vicious dog, I could probably outrun a prisoner. (I am just kidding.) I can't recall when or how he was recaptured, but I believe it was years later.

Another interesting but troubling fact about the road I walked on my way to school was that there was a creek without a bridge. This creek, although small, got wide and deep when it rained—up to our knees. Since now I was wearing shoes, I had to take them off, along with my socks, to cross over the creek, having to put them back on after crossing it. This was one of the most interesting stories of my young life.

I was also concerned about my parents because I knew they worried about my safety. The situation was difficult for me because there were no means of communication between my parents and me from early in the morning when I left for school until the early evening when I returned home from school. There were reasons for my concern for my parents, and reasons for my parents to worry about my safety.

I graduated from junior high school with the second highest grades of the class, and I continued my crusade onto high school. For another three years, I would be walking miles along a dangerous road. The high school was yet farther from home than the junior high school, but there was some transportation, which was some relief although it only went a short distance. Although the bus fare was only five cents, my parents could not afford it. So based on my high grade average, the government of Puerto Rico granted me financial help. High school was not difficult for me because I was used to similar challenges, including the crossing of the creek without a bridge.

While I was in high school, something happened that turned my life around; I met my first boyfriend. His name was Peter, and he seemed charming. He was attractive and had a friendly personality. Now I was creating new problems and a different kind of struggle for myself. And I had no doubt I had to hide it from my parents for my own good. Their philosophy was very simple: "No boyfriends while still in school, because it could affect your schoolwork." Changes in my lifestyle were happening quickly. And what I mean by "changes happening" was the fact that, knowing my parents' philosophy relating to boyfriends while in school, there was no way I was going to let them know about Peter. I was also fully aware of what my sisters had gone through with my parents after my parents learned about their relationships with boys.

Had my parents known, it would have been impossible for me to keep my boyfriend, my sanity, and especially, to keep being the caliber of student that I had always been. I was confident that I could do it my way without complicating matters. I was no longer the smart little girl without shoes. I had developed into an attractive young woman and was still smart. For me, there was no turning back and no chance to remain naïve and detached; to accept changes was not a choice. I had already created my own lifestyle, and against all odds, I was going to make it work for me. Of course, I was not about to let my schoolwork fall apart, nor to ignore my principles. I graduated from high school with honors, and without losing my boyfriend.

To New York

I graduated from high school in May 1953, and soon after left my home in the mountains of Yabucoa, Puerto Rico. On July 6, I left home for New York City in search of a job and my independence. My brother Fausto, who had been living in New York for a while, made my trip to New York possible by paying the forty-five dollars for my airline fare. Some of my friends thought my relationship with Peter would end after a long separation. But that never crossed our minds. We knew how much we loved each other.

My school years were over, but Peter had one more year to complete his. We both understood it was going to be almost impossible to see each other if I remained home. The reasons were obvious: my home was far from the city, and there was no transportation nearby, and every one of us siblings needed our parents' permission before leaving the house. For Peter, seeing me would have been just impossible. Unlike my parents, his did not prevent him from going anywhere. However, he knew coming by my house would mean trouble with my parents.

We were not worried about our relationship because it was strong enough to last. But not seeing each other was going to be difficult. I remember what he used to say when we talked about it: "Don't worry, honey, a year is not a long time. Before we know it, we will be together again." I just said, "I hope you are right, sweetheart." And he was right.

When I told my parents that I was leaving home for New York, they were not happy with my decision. They tried to change my mind so I could go to college. Father spoke to me with sadness and disappointment. He told me, in his own words, "If you don't further your education, you will be a wasted brain." I did not know what to say because I understood his disappointment with me. He wanted me to continue my education. I remained quiet as he added, "After you are gone, let's see which one of these guys who are after you will follow you to New York."

I suspected that my parents had an idea about my relationship with Peter during my high school years. Though I didn't know where their idea had come from, I believed it came from Peter. He had a friendly approach to people, and perhaps Father had noticed Peter being too friendly with him. Since Father knew who Peter's father was and they were not friends, Peter's friendliness with him seemed strange to my father. He thought Peter was looking for something, and it had to be me. However, my parents were not sure because they had never seen us together. I knew Father was watching me, and I never gave him a chance to catch us together.

On several occasions I had seen Father before he had seen me. When I walked over to greet him, Father said to me nicely, "I am sorry, my dear, but with that school uniform you all look alike." It was of dire importance for me not to let Father catch us together, so I promised myself not to let it happen. Peter had no knowledge of what was going on because we never talked about it and I did not want him to know. I was concerned about him getting upset, making the situation more complicated for the two of us.

I imagine some of my stories might be hard for some readers to believe, and I understand. But I can tell you that it was not as bad as it sounds. Using my 1953 graduating class as an example, I say this: there were fifteen honor students in this class, including me. Every one of us was highly successful reaching our goals, becoming schoolteachers, managers, doctors, engineers, and more. I don't remember how many students were in the class, but my guess is about one hundred. And not only the honor students made it; the rest of the class made it also. My point is these students, including me, did very well after experiencing such a difficult lifestyle. This indicates the lifestyle was not as unendurable as it appears to have been.

If I could only have the readers follow me to some of these events that happened over sixty years or more back, I daresay they would like to follow me a second time. I am not implying that I would choose to go back to that lifestyle if given the choice to stay where I'm now or to go back. Of course I would not go back, and I will tell you why. When comparing that time with today, you will discover in hindsight that no one works hard today; some people today don't even have to work to survive. Now I ask you, would you move from a place where you don't need to work hard for a living, to a place where you must work hard to make it? I think I know your answer. Those who endured that lifestyle, as I did, know what life is all about. They are proud of their achievements, especially the fact that they worked hard for it.

Father always came to town on his horse, and since I was familiar with the horse's gallop, I always knew when he was approaching us. I was certain that because my parents knew who Peter's father was, they would never agree to our relationship, which would have made it difficult for Peter and me to stay together. Our two families were members of different political parties, and politics played an important role in their lives. Peter's family belonged to the Socialist Party, in which they were actively involved in political activities. My family belonged to the Democratic Party and was also actively involved in political activities. Furthermore, my parents believed that a mountain girl was no match for a city boy, and they took it for granted that Peter was not for me. Therefore, after Father knew for sure that I was not changing my mind, as a small consolation for himself, Father thought it was better for me to go to New York, leaving the boys behind.

I never knew as a fact how or when Father discovered my relationship with Peter. But I know it was after I had left home. He never had a chance to say anything directly to me about Peter. I never mentioned his name to my family and kept our relationship as secret as possible. My parents never said and never asked me anything about Peter either, for they had no evidence to prove our relationship. However, Peter's family knew almost everything about it and would have done anything to stop it. And it was not because of me personally, but because of who my father was and where I was coming from, being from a rural community.

The reasons were obvious: the two families were well-known and respected in and out of town, in politics our families were called adversaries, Peter and I were raised in different lifestyles, and both families were financially well established. Peter's father, Don Polo Gomez, and my father treated each other like true politicians. Whenever they met, almost always, this is what they said to each other: "Como esta usted, Don Polo?" (How are you?) "Muy bien, Don Narciso. (Very well). Y usted, como esta?" "Estoy muy bien. Gracias a Dios." (Very well. Thank God.)

Peter's family was not against the relationship; they were against who the relationship was with. Peter was allowed to have relationships with girls, but not with Don Narciso's daughter, since Don Narciso was from the opposing political party. They didn't know me well, but they knew who Father was and that I was from the mountains. This was a time when city residents considered themselves, socially and financially, above rural residents. I would like readers to keep in mind that these events happened over sixty years ago, when women's rights did not exist.

Neither of our families was ready to welcome our relationship for several reasons. Politics, as I previously mentioned, was one of the reasons, but there were others. Peter's home was near the school and I had to pass by it on my way to and from school. I rarely stopped by his house because I thought that was the right thing to do. It was something that I had observed at home during my younger years. My parents applied to my sisters the same rules their own parents had applied to them when they were young. I did not want to go through that. According to my parents, the girl should visit the boy only on special occasions. They believed the boy should visit the girl at her home, almost always on Sundays. Peter's family, unaware of these rules, believed that I was unsociable.

I never doubted Peter's love for me. And regardless of the stories mentioned, we never let anything interfere with our relationship. He had no problem accepting me the way I was. He understood the way I was raised, even though it was very different from his. Peter also recognized that I was an intelligent and respected young woman with a bright future ahead. Some of Peter's most unforgettable actions demonstrating how much he cared for me bring me back to the sugarcane plantations and the creek without a bridge. Several times during stormy weather, Peter walked with me for miles along the dangerous road through the plantations. One of my most interesting experiences was when he carried me in his arms across the creek. He was aware of my struggles during bad weather, so he took it upon himself to walk with me for miles and to help me across the creek. Actions like these cannot be forgotten.

My school years were complete, but Peter had one more year to complete his. Aware of this, we planned for our future together before I left my home. Secretly planning for our future together made my mind wander. I could not help thinking about what I would be leaving behind and what my life would be like in the big metropolis, New York City.

Finally I found myself sitting on a plane for eleven hours trying to comprehend the actions and decisions I had recently made. This was difficult and overwhelming for me, but I never lost hope that everything was going to be all right.

I had not seen my sister Rose for many years. After an eleven-hour flight, it felt great to hear her voice when she said, "Hello, sister, how are you? You look good." I don't remember what I said to her. But she understood how tired I was. Rose is a lovely person who makes you feel relaxed. She looked at me and said, "Relax, we can talk when you feel better. The important thing is that you are here." I just said to her, "You make me feel good."

Rose was living in a quiet residential area, where all you could see were big buildings. Nothing seemed strange to me because I knew it was New York. I was feeling good and happy to be with Rose; but my heart was still in Yabucoa with the loved ones that I had left behind, especially Peter.

Shortly after I left home, Father received a letter from the University of Puerto Rico informing me of my acceptance to the university and of the registration dates. One more time Father asked me to return home to go back to school, but I chose not to go back. Father sent me the letter with a note. In the letter he said this: "I don't expect you coming back, but I will ask you anyway." I wrote him a letter thanking him for sending me the letter from the university and telling him not to worry about me because I was doing fine. I also told him that being with Rose was a pleasure because she was so good and beautiful.

In the meantime, for the one-year period before Peter could come to New York, Peter and I had agreed for my best friend Talma (now deceased) to take Peter's letters and send them to me as if they were her own. I was living with my sister Rose, and I had not told her about Peter for fear about my secret relationship being discovered and getting in trouble with my family. Peter wrote to me so often that to avoid arousing anyone's curiosity, Talma put several letters together and sent them to me as one. Reading his letters made me feel as if he were close to me. In his letters, unless there was something he thought I should know of, he only talked about the two of us. I could hardly keep up with him reading and answering his letters, for I didn't want anyone to know our secret.

In his letters, Peter never indicated anything other than his love for me. In fact, he appeared ready to come to me at any moment. Often he wrote, "Honey, I can't wait to see you. Time doesn't seem to be going fast enough for me." His only complaint was that I didn't write to him as often as he did to me. As for me, in my letters I always told him how much I loved him and missed him. Sometimes when he wrote, he said, "I know Talma is watching me. I better be good."

Soon after I arrived in New York, my brother Fausto and his friend Louis rented an apartment, and the three of us moved in. From then on, Peter was able to send his letters directly to me. I had told Fausto about my relationship with Peter, and it was okay with him. Our long-distance romance continued for the one-year period, and Peter and I were hoping for a happy ending. Our letters demonstrated a true love story. I kept our letters until 2006, when I purchased the house where I'm living now. At this point in my life, keeping the letters made no sense to me. They were in Spanish, and my children could not read them.

Readers might be misled by my secret actions and believe that I was disrespectful to my parents. Thus, I must explain to them the reasons for my behavior and my decision to not let my parents know about my relationship with Peter. I want readers to know the purpose behind what I did, and most of all to understand that at no time was my intention to disrespect my parents. I felt that at nineteen years of age, I was old enough to take control of my life, and I wanted to prevent conflicts between the families from further complicating the situation. I knew a decision had to be made, so I decided to do it my way, hoping to benefit everyone.

My parents had experienced my older sisters doing similar things, so it seemed to me that not letting them know about my relationship with Peter was the right thing to do. My choices did not create hardship for anyone, but if my parents had made the decisions for me, the effects would have been difficult for me to face and created unavoidable hardship for my parents. I will tell you what I mean by creating hardship. I knew my parents well. When they believed something was wrong, they didn't give up until they fixed it. Obviously, my parents would have believed my relationship with Peter was wrong and they had to fix it. But there was only one way for them to fix it, which was forcing me to end my relationship with Peter. If this had happened, the results would have been devastating and heartbreaking for Peter and me, and a self-created hardship for my parents.

Looking for Work and Finding It

Days after I arrived at my sister Rose's house, she went with me to look for a job. We went to a ladies' dress factory, where I met Tina, the supervisor. I had never met her before, but Rose knew her well. Tina was happy to meet me and happy to hire me. She knew my older sisters and was aware that all of them, as well as Mother, knew how to sew very well and were responsible people. She explained to me what the work was like and that it was piecework. I had never heard about piecework before, but I was excited because I had found my first job. Tina told me that I could start the next day.

I didn't know what piecework meant, and I asked Tina to explain it to me. She told me that I would be given a bundle of dresses already cut, for me to put them together at twenty-nine cents each. At the end of the day, the finished dresses were individually counted for each employee. At the end of the week, each employee was paid the number of dresses she had put together times twenty-nine cents.

I reported to work the next day, and the excitement about my first job quickly vanished. As soon as I heard the sewing machines going so fast, I knew the job was not for me; but I stayed until the end of the week. Then Tina said to me: "You earned only $4.80 for the week, but I'm giving you $5.00." I thanked her for giving me a chance and told her I was leaving. She felt sorry for me and said, "You did a good job on the few dresses that you put together, so perhaps you can develop some speed as you continue sewing." I knew that was not going to be the case with me; I thanked her again, said good-bye, and left. I was not surprised about my earnings because I have always been slow. Besides, I'm talking about things that occurred sixty years ago.

I went looking for work again, and I was hired at a stencils factory. This was a simple, but interesting, job. Some readers might not be familiar with stencils or what they were used for; I'm not sure if they are still on the market. A stencil is (or was) a metal product, gold-like in color, with letters or objects cut through. It was used in printing for making special lettering. When the product came out of the machine that made it, it was immersed in a liquid for luster before being put through the printing machine, which printed whatever was cut through the stencil. My job was immersing the stencils in the liquid. And my salary was twenty-nine dollars a week.

I liked the job and I was doing well. Then I signed a petition to join a labor union and got laid off. I started to collect unemployment, but one day I forgot to report to the unemployment office to sign in for the next month and I lost my right to collect. At that time, one had to report to the unemployment office in person once a month to sign in for the following month. I went back to looking for a job again.

In early 1954, I was hired by George McKibbin and Son, a bookbinding company. Finally, the stressful and tiring experiences of my six and a half months in New York had ended. From the first day on this job, I knew I was going to like it. The place was huge. This company occupied an entire floor in a multifloor building. I don't remember the floor we were on, but I still remember the address: 37 Thirty-Fourth Street, in the Bush Terminal industrial area of Brooklyn. This company's main function was bookbinding and printing. There were machines for all aspects of bookbinding and printing.

After the printing machine did the printing, the folding machine did the folding of the pages, now called signatures, which were taken to the gathering machine, also called the power collator. Once the book had been put together, it was taken to the sewing section. Here the sewing machine operator, keeping the book in order, fed the individual signatures to the sewing machine. The signatures were sown together, making a complete book. The employee who separated the books as they came out of the machine was called the "cutter-off." And that was my job. After I separated the books, I carried them to a flat bed, known as a "skid." Then I piled them up on the skid alternating their direction so they would not fall off when the skid was moved.

After being a cutter-off for some time, I was promoted to a sewing machine operator. This was a good place to work. Supervisors and coworkers were friendly. Some workers complained about working too hard, but it didn't bother me because I had worked hard since my childhood. I don't recall what my salary was at the beginning, but after ten years when the place closed, my pay was fifty-six dollars a week.

This industrial site comprised a number of strong, well-constructed buildings from, as far as I know, the forties and fifties. They represented the time when the manufacturing industry was going strong. Then came the sixties, and slowly but surely, the industry began to disappear.

While all of the above was happening, other interesting experiences were taking place in my life. I consider them interesting because at that time, women's rights were limited, and Hispanic women's rights were almost unheard of. This is one of the main reasons I wrote this book: to share my experiences with readers so they can keep them in mind if they are faced with similar situations in their lives. Women are better off today than during my younger years, but they often experience some degree of inequality.

Besides the struggles that I faced, I still had time to make new friends and have some fun. While working in the bookbinding shop, I met some young boys and girls, and we became good friends. They were young adults who enjoyed life and clean fun. On hot summer days, we went to Sunset Park in Brooklyn, and we spent hours together. We played games, went swimming and bicycle riding, and simply enjoyed being together and carefree. We all had respect for each other and valued our friendship.

I can honestly say that at this time I enjoyed some of the best moments of my young life. I liked my job and had good friends. Some of my male friends had a special interest in me, but I made sure I let them know about Peter. I told them that I valued their friendship and would like for us to maintain it even after Peter arrived, and so we did. The lesson I would like to convey to the reader is that although the truth might be hard to accept by someone and telling the truth could hurt a person's feelings, honesty is a wonderful thing. It is something that should be practiced in every kind of relationship. Honesty is a sign of integrity and trustworthiness. However, we must keep in mind that when facing an uncommon situation, one must apply common sense. For example, if telling the truth creates a serious disturbance or a dangerous situation, applying common sense could help you to decide what is best for all and prevent further complications.

Peter Arrives in New York

Peter graduated from high school in May 1954, and as previously planned, he left home for New York City. He went to live with his sister in the Bronx because he did not have any relatives in Brooklyn. This represented a great inconvenience for him because of the significant distance between the Bronx and Brooklyn. But against all odds, he managed to find his way to come to see me. I can't remember accurately how long after his arrival from Puerto Rico he came to visit me, but it was like on the next day. We were both happy and excited about seeing each other again. However, our excitement about being together was short lived; we had no idea of what we were to face soon.

Mother, who was visiting my sisters who were living in New York, was staying at my sister Rose's house at the time. When she learned that Peter was in New York and was visiting me, Mother moved in with me. She wanted to be present during his visits to me. I never learned how Mother found out that Peter was seeing me. But it had been going on for so long and so many relatives and friends knew about it, anyone could have told her, even someone still in Puerto Rico. At that time, Yabucoa was a very small town, where people knew each other. Besides, Peter and Father were both well-known in town. So I didn't think it was difficult for Father to find out about Peter and me.

I was living with my brother Fausto, but that did not matter to her. She knew Fausto worked at night and was hardly ever at home. Mother could not accept my relationship with Peter, and this created problems and conflicts in our relationship. According to Mother, we were too young to understand what a serious commitment was like; Peter was twenty and I was twenty-one years old. In spite of the difficult circumstances, I could not disrespect Mother. Needless to say, the situation was getting complicated and unbearable for me.

None of the ten children in our family, regardless of our ages, ever disrespected our parents. Challenging or arguing with Mother never happened. This was something I had learned during childhood, and it continued unchanged during adulthood. When she moved in with me, Mother made it clear that she did not approve of my relationship with Peter, and she would not leave until I decided what to do about it. Mother would not change her mind. She said she wanted me to solve the matter soon, for my own benefit. At this point my relationship with Peter was not going well. I was concerned about the fact that he did not want to talk about anything but the two of us. He acted as if everything were fine, when in reality, the situation was difficult and seriously complicated for the two of us. He was excited about getting married, and didn't seem concerned about our lives thereafter. I was concerned about his naive attitude.

Peter and I were working together, and so we were able to talk about our situation away from the family. After several stressful conversations with him, I decided to end our relationship. Peter refused, saying, "Don't even think about it because it is not going to happen." Our only other choice was to get married, so Mother could leave and we could go on with our lives together. Mother never interfered with any of her children's married lives once they were married. But the situation was taking a toll on me, and my mental stress had reached its highest level. I chose to get married, but I was not confident that I was doing the right thing. What if Mother were right? If so, I would have to take responsibility for my actions and face the consequences for my mistakes.

Mother was expecting my response, and I did not hesitate in giving it to her. I respectfully approached her and said, "Mother, I made my decision." She looked at me and said, "Yes, what is it?" When I told her, "I am going to marry Peter," it seemed to me she was expecting something else from me—a decision not to get married. After a moment of silence she told me, "If that's what you want, go ahead, but it doesn't make me happy." She reminded me what she had told me before, that both of us were too young to make serious commitments without giving thought to future disappointments.

I don't remember how much longer after we spoke Mother stayed with me, or how soon after, she went back home to Puerto Rico. I knew I did not have to worry about Father, for he was the opposite of Mother. He could adjust to any situation, so I believed I could do the same. I knew I had to make a difficult decision one way or the other. And I did it without thinking what might, or might not, happen in the future. What I do know for sure is Mother was not at the wedding.

MY WEDDING

On Valentine's Day, 1955, Peter knocked on my door. When I opened it, he gave me an engagement ring without stepping inside my apartment. I don't recall what we said to each other; all I remember is what he said: "Happy Valentine's Day, honey." Then he left. He knew Mother was with me, and he did not want to worsen the situation for me.

We set the wedding date for July 2, 1955. A few days before the wedding, my coworkers had a small party for me and gave me nice gifts. We had no money to pay for anything fancy, so I rented my wedding gown for thirty-five dollars to save some money to pay for a limousine to take us to the church. The wedding took place in an evangelical church in the Bronx, near Peter's sister's apartment. I don't remember the name of the church. It was a small wedding, and Peter and I were very happy together. There were no bridesmaids, just a maid of honor, a best man, and a flower girl. We had a small celebration at the maid of honor's apartment in the Bronx, and we all had a good time.

Then it was time to go home, which was my apartment in Brooklyn. We could not afford a limousine to take us back to Brooklyn. But, no, we did not have to stay in the Bronx. We took my favorite transportation, the New York City subways. Thank heavens for subways. Irene, one of my coworkers who attended the wedding, took the train with us for the one-and-a-half-hour train ride from the Bronx to Brooklyn. And yes, Mother had gone back home to Puerto Rico, though I don't remember exactly when.

The train ride was fun; we were feeling good and happy. Irene had a good sense of humor and made us laugh when she said to me, "You should have left your wedding gown on. It would have been much more fun." We had a few good laughs. And after all the struggles and stressful situations, Peter and I were ready to start a new life. My brother Fausto had moved out, and we had the apartment for ourselves.

MARRIED LIFE

When Peter and I got married, I had been working at the book factory for over a year. My coworkers and supervisors liked me and thought highly of me. There were a few Hispanic employees; all were men except for I and another woman, whose name was also Emma. After the wedding Peter would be living in Brooklyn. So I spoke to Mr. Monroe, my boss, and asked him if he could hire Peter. His response was to bring him in. Mr. Monroe was a respected man, who had silver hair and was getting along in years. The employees hardly spoke to him because he was strict and unfriendly. He never made friends with the workers. However, he always said hello to me and often asked me how I was doing.

Peter started to work with us, and all the workers were pleased to meet him and welcomed him. There was a lady named Kitty, who did not get along with anybody else but a woman called Catherine and me. The coworkers called her an "old maid," but she liked me and did not want anyone else to be her helper except me. When she met Peter, she liked him and often brought him white sweat socks to keep his feet cool in hot weather. Kitty always gave me good advice. She often brought me pieces of clothing and the lipstick color she suggested I wear to look prettier. She was intelligent, but lonely, and had only two friends, Catherine and me. Catherine used to tell me how much Kitty wished I were her daughter.

At the beginning our marriage was going well; we were both well liked and had good jobs and good friends. People used to call us the perfect couple. We became members of a Baptist church and were baptized together on Easter Sunday. I had been baptized in the Catholic church when I was a child because my family was Catholic. But I never went to church. Unfortunately, less than six months after our wedding, Peter made a big mistake that tarnished our relationship forever.

It was Christmastime, and we had purchased new outfits to wear on our first Christmas together. We had no specific plans on what to do or where to go on that day. I thought we should visit a friend nearby and enjoy being together, but Peter had other plans. He asked me to go with him to his sister's house in the Bronx—a train ride over an hour long. I told him I did not feel like going that far, especially at night when train service was less frequent. To my surprise, his response was, "If you do not go with me, I will go by myself." And he left, leaving me alone on our first Christmas.

I did not know what to say or what to do, and cried in disbelief. Suddenly there was a knock on the door, and I thought it must be Peter coming back to be with me. I quickly dried my tears and opened the door. It was Louis, a friend of ours who had come to invite us to the house of another friend who was having a party. Louis looked at me, noticed that I'd been crying, and asked me, "Where is Peter?" And I told him what had happened. Louis could not believe Peter was capable of doing something like that to me. He knew how much Peter loved me.

Louis thought that Peter must have been joking. After waiting a while for him to return, Louis said, "I am not leaving you alone. If you do not go with me to my friend's party, I will stay with you until Peter returns. He is not worthy of you." I just said, "Okay." So I went with Louis to the other friend's party. Some of my friends were there having a good time, and I tried to look happy. Meanwhile, Louis was watching me, and he noticed that I was not comfortable being there. He came over and asked me, "Do you want to go home?" I said, "Yes," and we left. I could not get Peter off my mind, and silently I kept wondering what could be going through his mind. How had he dared to do this to me? I remembered something my parents had said to me: that Peter was not for me. Louis had meant the same thing when he said Peter was not worthy of me.

I returned home after midnight, and soon after, Peter came back. I had advised Louis to leave quietly after Peter returned to avoid a possible confrontation with him. Louis left without saying a word. I chose to keep quiet, though from then on, I was concerned about our relationship. Peter remained silent as if waiting for me to start questioning him. I knew the most painful struggle of my lifetime had just begun. I was facing a situation in which I had no choice and would have no help from anyone. I was on my own.

Once again I thought about my parents' wisdom and the lessons I had learned during my childhood. These were the only tools I had to help me go on living a normal life, or at least pretending to be normal. Somehow, I managed to overcome the problems and went on with my life without saying anything to anyone. I often thought about another thing my parents had told me: that we were too young to understand such a serious commitment or to take responsibility for our mistakes, regardless of their nature. Now I had to painfully accept that my parents had been right. I never mentioned my problems to my family, letting them believe that we were the perfect couple. To pretend that I was enjoying my married life was easy for me because Peter was friendly and nice to my family. Unaware of what was going on, my family loved him.

What Peter did on our first Christmas bothered me for a very long time. And it seemed to me he thought nothing of it. Obviously, a trip to the Bronx had not been previously planned. When we purchased the outfits, we both understood they were for our first Christmas together. He never mentioned to me going to the

Bronx, though he knew I never enjoyed going there. Also, he was aware that during night hours, train service was slow and it was cold. Peter never said he was sorry, and we never talked about it again. But how could a newlywed young man do such a thing to his bride on their first Christmas together? It was no secret that we loved each other, unless I had been dreaming all that time.

To this day, I have not been able to understand why he did it. Peter acted cold, something I don't believe he was; and he acted selfish and with no regard for my feelings. And there is one more thing that I would like to add: Peter was told that I was writing a book, perhaps by a family member. And recently, I called him to let him know that Peter Jr. was retiring and he was welcome to the party. Here is what he said to me, among other things: "If Peter wants me to go to his party, let him tell me, not you. And by the way, I don't care what you write in the book. Write whatever you want." My response was, "I see you have not changed; but don't worry, you will not hear from me again." I told Peter Jr. about it, and he said, "I don't know why you bother with him. I don't need him; I have you."

Amid all our ups and downs, we never argued. If we disagreed on something, we talked about it in a friendly manner. Ironically, I never doubted Peter's love for me; he just went about it the wrong way, thinking about satisfying his needs while ignoring mine. Perhaps, although this happened during the mid-fifties, he was still living decades back when "she" had to do what "he" said. It seemed to me that he thought love was a one-way street, and that going only his way was good for both of us. After we were together almost two years, something happened that turned our lives around one more time.

PETER JR. IS BORN

We were living in a furnished apartment at 691 Sixth Avenue in Brooklyn, New York, where I had been living for some time before getting married. (The building has since been torn down.) Furnished apartments were the norm for the time. Peter and I were doing fine, enjoying new friends and doing well in our jobs. We both had been promoted to better-paid positions and were saving money. Now I was a machine operator rather than a helper.

The news that we were expecting a baby brought excitement and a special feeling of happiness to us like never before. Peter and I were extremely happy about the baby and quickly started to look for an unfurnished apartment. To find an apartment at that time, in the late fifties, was fast and easy. Homeowners and landlords displayed signs for "furnished" and "unfurnished" apartments on the windows, instead of using real estate services. It was a good practice because you saved money and were able to look around the area without being distracted by real estate agents.

Sometime in the summer of 1956, we moved to an unfurnished, two-bedroom apartment in a three-family house. To our surprise, the house was owned by a Puerto Rican couple, Angela and Antonio. He was a merchant marine who almost always was at sea in a commercial boat. Since he was seldom home, Dona Angela, as everyone called her, was in charge. The way in which she interviewed us made me think that she was not a nice person. Peter did all the talking while I remained quiet. I noticed she seemed to like Peter and rarely looked at me. After talking to him for a while, she looked at me and said this: "I do not want children in the apartment. I want you to know that." I remained quiet because I was three months pregnant.

The house was a very well-kept frame house painted gray. It was not a new house, but since it was so clean and neat, it was an attractive place to live. As for the apartment, it was in excellent condition. It had a big kitchen, a big bathroom, a small bedroom, and a spacious bedroom. Dona Angela made us aware of her rules for her tenants: no loud noise, no smoking, no parties, and no children. If children came to visit, they were not allowed in the hallways. She was happy to know we did not practice any of the things she had mentioned. Peter became her friend, but she disregarded me. I did not mind being overlooked because I liked the place. And perhaps the fact that she liked Peter could make it easier for Peter to tell her about the baby when the time came. She let us rent the apartment and said, "Rent is sixty dollars per month, and you must keep the place clean."

We had been saving money to buy some furniture and things for the baby. We purchased our first TV, a black and white console, and also a light-color, four-piece bedroom set and a small dinette. When Dona Angela came to look at the apartment for the first time after we had moved in, she was impressed because we were very neat and well organized. Three months after moving to the apartment, I started to show signs of my condition. By now I was six months into my pregnancy. One evening, when Peter and I were coming home from work, Dona Angela saw us and noticed I had gained weight. She approached me and asked me, "Are you pregnant?" I answered, "Yes." She got upset and asked me, "Why didn't you tell me so when you came to see the apartment?" I responded by saying, "I didn't know at the time." She did not believe me, but she let us stay anyway.

Meanwhile, there was a couple living in the apartment above us, Frank and Hazel, and we became friends. Hazel often told me stories about Dona Angela. According to her, Dona Angela was seeing a psychiatrist for a mental condition. She also said that I should be careful with my baby because Dona Angela was capable of kidnapping or hurting my baby if she did not like me.

When I mentioned my conversation with Hazel to Peter, he did not believe it, but I became concerned about the baby's safety. Dona Angela talked to Peter every time she had a chance. Since she liked him, I was hoping that she'd let us stay in the apartment after the baby was born. A few months went by, and I started feeling symptoms that the time was approaching. Peter was concerned about leaving me alone while he was at work, so he took me to my sister Rose's house. I remained there until the baby was born in January 1957.

New Struggles and Difficult Situations

I had never imagined the mental stress and the physical pain that I experienced after returning home with my child. My mental stress was created by several factors, the most worrisome one being my poor physical condition. The hours of severe pain experienced before and during giving birth, and the level of discomfort felt thereafter, had taken a toll on me. Sitting, walking, and picking up the baby were all extremely painful. I had become anemic and weak, and had to remain hospitalized for eight days.

Before I was discharged from the hospital, the doctor explained to me the things I should not do to keep from aggravating my condition. I was concerned about not being able to do at least the most necessary things around the house, for Peter had to go to work. But my biggest concern was Dona Angela after I came back home with the baby. Dona Angela, though she did not want tenants with children, often came to us to hold and play with the baby. She almost always talked to Peter, telling him how beautiful Little Peter was. I didn't trust her. I was afraid she wanted the baby to become familiar with her. And keeping in mind Hazel's stories about her, that was a bad sign for me.

Most of my feelings and concerns I kept to myself, because telling Peter would not do any good because he could not afford to stay home. But he tried to help me whenever he could. Regardless of my condition, there was one thing that kept me going and gave me strength: Little Peter, as he was being called. He was a strong, healthy, and beautiful baby who rarely cried, but had to be fed often, especially at night. As I watched him, I felt relaxed and confident that I was going to make it, because the love of my child would offset my stress and pains. I enjoyed watching him peacefully sleeping and waking up, waiting to be fed. Time went by, and Little Peter grew stronger and more beautiful, capturing everyone's love with his charm. Peter and I were proud of him and made sure we gave him all the love and care a child needs.

As for my family, the means of communication were very few. My parents were alone most of the time, for the children had gone their own way, and Mother could not write. Father always tried to keep in touch by writing, but it was not easy for him. However, we always found a way to contact them. Besides, they often came to visit for long stays.

My physical condition was slowly improving; just as the doctor had told me, it was going to take some time. He also told Peter that I needed to rest. I became attached to the baby and felt he eased my pains and discomfort. Unfortunately, I noticed Peter's attitude negatively changing. His behavior was disturbing, making the situation more difficult and more complicated for me to tolerate. He often asked me, "When are you going to be okay? Why is it taking so long for you to get better?" He asked me questions that I had no answers for. I tried my best not to let it get to me, and I remained calm to avoid a more serious situation.

I had heard people say that some men get jealous of their own children when too much attention is given to the children and not to them. I never thought it could be true, but now I had to believe that indeed it was true. With total disregard for my delicate condition and the love for our child, he told me, "Since the baby was born, your attention has been going to the baby and none to me." I do not remember what I said or what I did when he said that. He continued saying other things just as hurtful, and he asked me, "Is this what I deserve for loving you so much?"

Peter did not show any sign of regret for what he said. He acted rude and cold, something that was most disturbing to me. But one thing was clear to me: from that moment on, our relationship could never be the same. I managed to remain in control by applying a lesson learned from Mother: do not lose control in difficult situations if you want a positive ending to the matter. I knew I was alone in what was ahead for me, and I needed to set my priorities. I started to prepare myself for what could prove to be the most painful and difficult struggle of my married life.

As inconceivable as his behavior was, Peter did not believe that he was doing anything wrong. He thought that he was just letting me know how he felt about our situation. I began to understand what his problem could be. Once again, I thought about what my parents had tried to convey to me so many times before: that we were too young for serious commitments and that we were making serious decisions without thinking about what the future could be like. I also remembered the most important lesson from Mother during my childhood: that I must take responsibility for my actions, regardless of their nature and their outcome. Now I had to admit that my parents knew better. I can also cite something that I mentioned in my reasons for writing this book: "If I had known better."

I did not take too long to decide what to do; I would set my priorities and deal with them accordingly. I listened and observed Peter, and his lack of maturity came clearly to my mind. While my actions demonstrated maturity on my part, his had remained unchanged. It was obvious to me that his behavior was childish; it was clearly not his intention to hurt me or the baby in any way. He loved the baby and also loved me without a doubt. Knowing him and his background helped me understand who he really was. Peter was a good person and had a lot of love to offer, but he did not know how to go about it. By keeping that in mind and by looking at the small precious human being near us, I was confident that I could make it. I honestly thought that time would bring Peter some maturity to prevent similar incidents in the future—but I was wrong.

At times when I am alone, I ask myself why it took me so long to understand who Peter really was. And every time I try to find an answer, nothing seems right to me. Twenty-two years are seemingly a very long time. But understanding the circumstances, it might not be so. That was how long it took me to find out who Peter really was. And I don't regret it because it was for the sake of my children. And today, I am proud of my children.

Buying a Brownstone House

I consider buying a brownstone house my biggest bizarre achievement. How I was able to do it is so puzzling you could call it a miracle. I will try to explain to readers, to the best of my recollection, what happened and why I call it a miracle and bizarre. There are several factors and reasons for it.

Peter and I were looking for a bigger and more comfortable apartment. The idea of buying a house had never crossed our minds. However, when I told Kitty, the woman who was always helping me, that Peter and I were looking for a better apartment, she told me that it was not the right thing for me to do. She advised me to buy a house; not to look for an apartment. I thought she was kidding and said to her that I knew she was always wishing the best for me, but Peter and I did not have enough money to buy a house. Then she told me to go to a real estate office and talk to an agent, without wasting my time looking for an apartment.

Kitty always told me that I was a smart and good-looking young lady who deserved more than I was getting and that I could reach whatever I searched for. I took her advice and told Peter about it. He did not want to take that risky chance, but I convinced him to go with me to the real estate office. I was not too sure that we were going to get very far, for several reasons. Besides being Hispanic, we were very young—Peter was twenty-three and I was twenty-four years old—and we had been in New York less than six years. We had no knowledge about what a brownstone house was and were completely unaware of real estate values and of good or bad communities. As previously mentioned, Peter and I had been promoted to better-paid positions and we were saving money to move to a better apartment. To avoid possible complications, we had not told anyone we were planning to move out of Dona Angela's house.

We went to a real estate office and explained our situation to an agent, telling him we wanted to buy a house but that we had only about $2,300 in savings. He seemed impressed that we had that amount of money available. The agent mentioned to us some of the details involved in buying a house and the total amount of money that would be needed for the closing. He told us that for the house he was about to show us, the closing costs could be about $3,000. I was concerned because we did not have that amount of money available. He then talked to us about Park Slope and its brownstone houses and their value. I told him that it did not matter to us because we didn't have the amount of money required for the closing.

The asking price for the house we were viewing was $20,000, and though it might not sound like a lot of money today, in 1959 it was a lot. After listening to us telling him over and over again that we could not make it, the agent said we could make a deal. He lowered the price of the house to $19,500 so we could make it with the money we had. He took us to see the house, and what a disappointment that was! According to the agent, the house had been vacant for about two years, and it was an eyesore for the community. The front door was open and missing the doorknob, some windowpanes were broken, the façade was missing some pieces, and the side entrance was blocked by debris several feet high. Peter did not comment about the condition of the house, but I was already making plans in case the deal went through. I had already set up my mind to look for a house, not for an apartment.

I didn't ask to look at any other houses because I was sure we would not be able to meet the closing costs. The fact that I already knew we could make a deal with this one kept me from looking further. I didn't want to risk losing this property and not finding another affordable one. The condition of the building didn't concern me. I was aware of the task ahead of me, but I was certain that I could do it. As for the costly repairs, I was not concerned: we would take one step at a time. The good thing was that we could get out from Dona Angela's house to our own house.

The inside of the house was a mess, but I noticed the living room was big, and though full of trash, it was in fair condition and had a nice wooden floor. I was confident I could clean the mess to use the room until the rest of the house was cleaned and organized. After the walk-through, the agent told us that everything looked good, pending the background check and the mortgage approval. He said he would contact us on a later day with all the details. We could not afford a lawyer and were told that we could use their lawyer. He would prepare all the necessary documents for the closing.

I do not remember exactly how long we waited for the call, but the agent called us within a short period of time, giving us all the relevant information and the date for the closing. I was very nervous, but I kept it to myself. Peter was nervous too, but he kept quiet and we both did very well. Everybody seemed friendly and helpful, and we began to feel more relaxed. However, unknown to us, they had a reason for the friendly and cordial attitude they were showing us.

The lawyer's name was Murry Oko; the spelling might not be correct, but it is close enough. An event that happened fifty-five years ago is difficult to remember accurately, but I will try to explain it to readers to the best of my recollection. At the closing, everything was going well until we heard that we were short by $175.00. Peter and I just looked at each other without saying anything. Then we were told not to worry because the real estate company would lend us the money and we would pay them $20.00 a month, in addition to the mortgage payments of $132.00 monthly. Finally, after the document signing and the good luck and good wishes, we had purchased a brownstone house, and we still had $10.00 in the bank.

We purchased the house on November 19, 1959, and moved in two days later. As previously planned, we cleaned the living room and made space for all our personal things and some furniture. I have no recollection about how we brought the furniture over, but we did it all in two days. We were all happy, including Little Peter, who quickly got busy going up and down the stairs before falling asleep on the steps. He was almost three years old. We covered the broken window glass with cardboard and tied the front door with a string, for it did not have a lock.

There were a number of reasons why we were moving. Besides being concerned about the baby's safety due to Dona Angela's mental condition as Hazel had explained it to me, the main reason was that Dona Angela had given us thirty days to move out of her house. What happened was that Father, who was visiting me, was taking a bath, and a significant amount of water had fallen on the floor. The water had dripped down the wall into her living room, and obviously, she was very upset. When I told her about Father taking a bath, she responded by saying that he was not supposed to be with us and therefore we had thirty days to get out of her house. I told Peter about the incident, and he said that we had to get out as soon as possible. The next day at work, I told Kitty that I was looking for an apartment without telling her the reason why. It was then that she advised me to buy a house.

We told Dona Angela that we had purchased a brownstone house and we were moving before the thirty days she had given us to move out. She was surprised and could not believe it, and told us that she wanted to see the house. She knew what a brownstone house was and that the Park Slope community was considered one of the best and most expensive residential areas in Brooklyn— something we did not know. She came to visit, wished us good luck, and left. Thereafter we did not hear about her for a while. One day I met someone who knew her and told me that she had been admitted to a mental institution.

Some of the stories about our purchase are hard to believe. For example, some of my relatives felt sorry for me. They thought I had made a costly mistake purchasing such an old and dilapidated building. Like me, my relatives had no idea about the history and value of brownstone houses. The house was built in the late 1800s and had been neglected for several years. According to some longtime residents and community advocates, we were the third owners. My sister Juanita and her husband George (both deceased), who lived in New Jersey, came over to see the house. They brought with them a bed, a few chairs, a bag of groceries, and other items because they thought we had no money to buy food and furniture. Although that was not the case with us, we thanked them for their concern and generosity.

We started to take care of the most urgent repairs and were doing well. Ironically, and thanking my surreal and bizarre help coming from who knows where, I was prevented from making a terrible mistake. As stated earlier, there were several pieces missing from the façade of the building. Since there was no one to ask for advice and Peter and I did not know any better, I took it upon myself to find someone who could make the repairs, though I had just ten dollars in the bank. I knew it was going to be an expensive job, and I contacted several contractors for estimates. I chose a contractor who, after looking at the repairs to be made and the materials I had chosen, gave me a price of nine hundred dollars.

I knew that I had to get a loan, and I went to the Greater New York Savings Bank (no longer in business) and spoke to a loan specialist. I explained to him what the loan was for and that the property was a brownstone house. I also let him know that I had already agreed with a contractor on the cost for the repairs and on the materials to be used. When I mentioned to the specialist that aluminum siding would be installed on the entire façade of the building, he was skeptical about my story and said that he needed to see the house before approving the loan.

The specialist came to see the house and was surprised that a contractor would dare to do that kind of work on a brownstone house. He told me that kind of material was not right on a brownstone building, and therefore, he could not approve my loan. I wondered if that was the real reason for not giving me the loan, but I thanked him for his help and concern. Later on, after speaking with some of the neighbors, I learned that the loan specialist was correct and had saved me from practically destroying the building's façade. Moreover, I could have gotten in trouble with people in the community and with the city as well. Finally, and after I learned my lesson, the loan for nine hundred dollars was approved. Another contractor did the work with the right materials. The work was done professionally, the neighbors were happy, and so was the community.

Besides my comments above, I still have other interesting stories about the reasons why I call my buying-a-brownstone-house experience my most bizarre and like-a- miracle achievement. Some of the stories are unthinkable, and readers might find them beyond belief. Imagine a young couple like Peter and I, inexperienced and without money, purchasing a brownstone house in one of the best residential and most expensive communities in New York City. Furthermore, mortgage payments were never late, the mortgage was paid off in seventeen years, and several expensive repairs were made to the property. And we were able to accomplish all these events without money in the bank. The only things we had to show at that time were excellent recommendations from our employer and an almost perfect credit score. I believe these stories are unique and should be told for readers to be aware that there are ways to improve their quality of life if they really work hard for it.

I saved the best for last on my brownstone house story for a reason. And I hope readers, especially the younger ones, think of my experiences and use them to learn to trust and believe in themselves with conviction. Readers should keep in mind that for any kind of situation, there is a solution somewhere. Do not be afraid to make a decision or to make a mistake. If you do make a mistake, learn from it. We all make mistakes and bad decisions at one time or another during the course of our lives. I have been around for many years, and I am yet to meet someone who has never made a mistake or a bad decision. Believe me, I have made more than one myself, and I have learned from them. I can honestly say that while some people, including some of my relatives, thought I had made a terrible mistake when buying the old and dilapidated brownstone house, it turned out to be one of my best achievements.

The following incident is the most bizarre that I experienced when Peter and I purchased the house. Almost twenty years after buying the property, I found out what I believe the real estate company had in mind for us when we bought the house. According to articles I read in the daily newspapers, allegedly the company had been taking advantage of minority clients who were buying real estate. In my opinion, for I do not know how the case ended, they thought we were like other minority clients they had taken advantage of before. It seems to me they believed we were ignorant and did not know any better. Therefore, being ignorant, we would purchase the property but would not be able to maintain it; thus, we'd lose the property and it would go back to the seller. And that explains the friendly and cordial environment they offered us at the closing.

I believe incidents like these are still happening when dealing with minority clients in real estate property sales. In some cases, the seller, though aware that the client will not be able to maintain the property, makes it as easy as possible for the client to purchase it. Thereafter, the client fails in the commitment, and the property returns to the seller. This was not the case with us, but it gives me reason to believe that was what they had in mind for Peter and me when we purchased the brownstone house.

What the seller did about twenty years after we bought the property was absolutely bizarre, and like a miracle as well. Without any late payments, the mortgage was satisfied seventeen years after we had purchased the property. After we had satisfied the mortgage, we received a letter from the real estate agency claiming that we had not paid them back the $175.00 they lent us at the closing. They wanted us to send them a check for the full amount or to provide them with evidence that we had paid them in full.

I believe it was like a miracle because to find such evidence on something that happened over twenty years back was absurd and highly unlikely. To my surprise, I was able to find the tiny, dated money order stubs for the complete amount of the $175.00 in question. Finding these small pieces of evidence after over twenty years is beyond belief. One cannot help getting suspicious about these senseless actions. I suspect that they believed we were not academically prepared to deal with serious matters and did not know any better. Perhaps they thought that after such a long time, we would not find any evidence to prove we had paid them back the full amount. In my written response, I informed them that I had evidence to prove that we had paid them the full amount and that the evidence was available to them if they wished to come by and verify it. I did not hear from them again. After twenty years? If this is not bizarre, what is?

The story about their lawyer, Murry Oko, is quite appalling. I cannot recall the date accurately, but it was either shortly before or after the event of the $175.00 that I read a newspaper article about the real estate lawyer, Murry Oko. He had been accused of taking advantage of minority clients when dealing with home sales. I do not remember how the case ended, but as I mentioned earlier, I believe they had the same thing in mind for Peter and me when we purchased the house. It is difficult to ignore the obvious similarities between our bizarre experience when we bought the property in Park Slope and what the lawyer and the real estate company had been accused of.

Finally, I can proudly say that all the struggles and sacrifices experienced when purchasing my brownstone house became one of my biggest and most talked about achievements during my young life. I enjoyed the house for forty-five years, and some of them were the best years of my life. The house was one of the best maintained properties in the community, rather than an eyesore, as it had been in the past. In 2004, unwillingly, I sold my beautiful brownstone house due to personal reasons. Time changes, and so do we.

NEIGHBORS

When Peter and I purchased the brownstone house in Park Slope and moved in, we were unaware that we had become members of a tight community of homeowners. These homeowners were up to date on community issues and knew something that Peter and I had no clue about. We had been living near the Park Slope community for the six years we had been in New York City. However, we had no knowledge of anything about this community in particular. And we were not aware of the degree of concern we were causing some neighbors on the block. We were tirelessly cleaning the house and taking care of the most-needed repairs without realizing that some neighbors were watching us. They were not watching what we were doing; they were watching us. Their concern was about the people moving to their community, and they had reasons for their concerns. I will let readers know what the neighbors' reasons for concern were, and at the same time share a bit of community history about Park Slope for them to enjoy.

Park Slope is a residential community with a great history behind it. I previously stated that Peter and I purchased the house in late 1959. Unknown to us, this was a time when Park Slope was beginning one of its many historical changes. Historically, this community, regardless of its good and bad times, remains one of the best and most diverse and expensive areas in New York City. And keeping in mind that communities cannot make people, but people can make communities, you can understand the reasons for the neighbors' concerns when I moved to Park Slope. I consider this success story a miracle because after decades, I still wonder how I was able to accomplish so much with so little.

Our neighbors' worries and concerns could have been understood in two ways: positive or negative. According to some people we had been talking to, their main concern was the building maintenance by the new owners, something they thought in most cases was positive. In our case, their concern could be negative. They were having a hard time trying to figure out who we were and how we could improve a property in such poor condition. Unable to come to a comfortable conclusion, they watched us from behind their window blinds.

Six months after we moved in, everything was going well. The neighbors knew we were Hispanics, but were not too sure if we could take care of the most-needed repairs to the building. They were not as concerned as they were initially, and although their concern was dissipating, they kept watching us. And one day, seven months after we had moved to the neighborhood, an event took place that made all concerns vanish forever. It was my sister Margaret's wedding. The reason for our tireless work was that we were preparing the house for the wedding celebration. It was an unforgettable event. Some neighbors stood in front of their homes, waiting for the bride to come out. When she did, standing on the top step of the stoop, they were surprised at how beautiful she looked.

Everyone in the wedding party looked fine and well organized. The event, although small, was a success and enjoyed by all. Thereafter, some of the neighbors said to me that Margaret had been one of the most beautiful brides they had seen. Days after the event, an outspoken neighbor with a good sense of humor came to my house to talk to me. She asked me, "Would you mind if I tell you something I want you to know?" I said it was okay, and she started to tell me things that had both of us laughing.

She said this: "I want you to know why and how we have been watching you for a while. Since the neighbors could not tell what kind of people had just moved to the neighborhood, we had some concerns. Therefore, we watched you from behind the window blinds. But now that we know the kind of people you are, our concerns are gone and the neighbors are happy." We became the best of friends. To this day, some of my former neighbors believe I am a rich woman.

Everybody Needs Somebody

In 1965, I met the person who guided me along the road to success, upon which I never turned back. This incomparable person was Professor Pablo Ortiz-Cotto. And my story goes like this: One day I received a call from my sister Sylvia, who was doing some office work in my brother Nick's office at the University of Puerto Rico. She told me she had given my telephone number and my address to Professor Pablo Ortiz-Cotto, who was coming to New York, and I should expect his call.

My husband, Peter, and I had previously heard who this person was but had never met him. A few days later, Professor Ortiz called for directions on how to get to my house by taxi from JFK Airport. Shortly thereafter, he arrived at my house. He was happy to meet us, including my eight-year-old son, Little Peter. He thanked us for welcoming him to our home, and then he explained to us the purpose of his visit, which was to do research at several learning institutions for the completion of his thesis to earn his PhD in education.

Peter knew Pablo liked to talk about education. So he didn't have much to say because he was not interested in talking about going back to school. Instead, he enjoyed talking about the Yankees and other less important topics of everyday life. Peter's attitude was seemingly strange to Pablo, but at times he watched the Yankees games with Peter.

I could tell Pablo wanted to talk to me about going back to school. So one day during a conversation, he started by asking me, "What are your plans for the future?" He noticed that I didn't know what to say; I believe I said, "My future?" As the smart man he was, he recognized that I was going in the wrong direction. Then he asked, "Have you considered going back to school?" "How could I?" I said. "I have to take care of my son and my husband."

He listened to my reasons for not going back to school. As the main reasons, I mentioned my eight-year-old son, my husband, and my lack of experience in everything else but bookbinding. I had worked as a bookbinder for ten years. I also mentioned I might not feel comfortable in the school environment after being out for such a long time. And perhaps I might not be able to master the English language at the college level.

Without hesitation and in a simple and convincing manner, Pablo said, "I understand your concerns, but regardless, you need to further your education. And I am going to help you do so." He added, "You can overcome your fears and concerns because what you just said is not a problem. Little Peter is in school all day, and your husband can take care of himself. So you can attend school in the morning. As for the language, don't worry, because your English is better than that of many others I know." My response was, "I don't believe my husband is going to agree with my plans." That did not seem right to Pablo.

We then talked extensively about both of our families. Pablo knew my brother Nick well and thought highly of him. He was not surprised when he learned the kind of student I had been because he knew my family. However, he was surprised that I had not furthered my education, adding that he would talk to me about it later. Pablo told me how proud he was of his two sons and his two daughters. All four of them were professionals, especially his oldest son, who was a scientist.

I had been an "A" student through my school years and had endured difficult situations and experiences early in my life, but according to Pablo, the best of me was yet to come. Numerous times I had been told that I was wasting my time and brain, though I had the potential to do a lot better. However, I still could not see the light at the end of the tunnel.

I was about to begin a new chapter in my life with new challenges, greater sacrifices, and conflicts at home, for my husband wanted me to stay home. Meanwhile, Pablo had been searching for a learning center where I could register as soon as possible because he had to return to Puerto Rico. We went to a training institute in downtown Brooklyn (I do not recall the name) where I registered for a six-month typing and keypunch course, from September 1965 to February 1966.

This time I knew I would not be an "A" student because of my lack of speed. And although I was one of the best in accuracy, I could not improve my speed and continued typing with two fingers, never learning the keyboard. The instructor did not believe the lack of speed was a problem because I had accuracy, and speed could increase with practice. Students with too many errors would not earn the certificate of completion regardless of their speed.

Soon the course was near its end and we were to have the final test. But I did not have to worry about failing the test because I had been hired by a federal agency. I would be starting my new job one month before the course completed. The instructor was happy for me and gave me the certificate of completion, saying that I would do well anywhere I went because of my accuracy.

Pablo returned to Puerto Rico happy that I had gone back to school and confident that I would continue to further my education. Thereafter I did not see him again for several years. From time to time, he came to New York for personal matters, and he always took time to visit me. And during my trips to

Puerto Rico, I visited him, and then he accompanied me to see my family up in the mountains of Yabucoa. My parents were fond of Pablo. We kept in touch by telephone or by mail.

My stories give credence to what we often hear people say: "Everybody needs somebody." In 1965, I met that somebody, Professor Pablo Ortiz-Cotto. This man was a remarkable human being. Sylvia knew him well, and she was certain I would be proud to have him staying in my house. Meeting Pablo was one of the most important events in my life. Had it not been for Pablo, I would not be sitting here today writing my book. And my college education, rather than an achievement, would have been a lifelong dream, or as Father had said, a "wasted brain."

In January 1966, Jose, a former coworker from the bookbinding company, came to visit me. I had not seen him since the company had closed a couple years earlier. Since I was not working, he provided me with a job application from the federal agency he was working for, which was the General Services Administration, known as GSA. The next day, Monday, January 31, 1966, I went to apply for a job in person. During the interview I explained in detail my experience on bookbinding and my lack of speed on typing; I also mentioned my accuracy.

The interviewer was impressed with my honest and detailed answers to his questions. He told me there were two vacancies, a typist and a bookbinder, and I was qualified for both. But as a procedure, he had to test me on typing and keypunching. Needless to say, I failed both. But it did not matter because I was hired as a bookbinder, reporting to work the next day. And on February 1, 1966, I started to work for GSA, at a salary of ninety-six dollars a week.

A few years later, Pablo came to visit me again. He was convinced that I was doing the right thing, attending school pursuing a college degree. Meanwhile, I was beginning to understand the point Pablo was trying to convey to me: that without a college degree, I would remain where I was indefinitely.

Pablo enjoyed helping people in need, regardless of who they were or where they came from. During Christmastime, we always wrote a happy message in the cards we sent to each other. In his 2011 Christmas card (his last Christmas), he wrote in his message that he was going to write me a long letter telling me about "the tragedy of my life." I never received his letter, and I never knew what he meant by the "tragedy of my life." Then I heard how seriously ill he was, and suddenly I felt a deep pain in my heart and tears in my eyes. Unfortunately, there was nothing that I could have done for him at the time. Since I had been told that he could move his eyes and could read, I wrote him a note and mailed it to him, hoping someone would bring it to his bed. And I trust somebody did. On September 4, 2012, he left this world and the people he loved, with his beloved family by his side.

My only consolation after his passing was the note I had sent to him. I wanted him to know my true feelings for him and how grateful I was for all he had done for me. I would like to share my note with readers so they can understand why I feel the way I feel about this remarkable man. This is what I wrote to him:

> February 2, 2012
>
> Pablo, your serious health condition saddens and concerns me greatly. I want you to know that I always think of you and that I pray to God to keep you pain-free, while filling your heart with peace and tranquility. You deserve no less. I will never forget the incomparable and professional help and advice you gave me when I needed it the most. Your unconditional help motivated me to reach my goals further than I expected. I will remember you forever. I am planning on writing a book

about my life, and if I do, I will dedicate it to you. I know you will not be able to reply to this short message, but it doesn't matter; I just want you to know the influence you had on my professional life and how grateful I am for all you did for me and some of my loved ones. God will compensate you for all your deeds. The enclosed pictures, I hope, will bring a special moment of happiness to "The Patita Man." The child is beautiful and very smart. Thank you again for what you did for me and my loved ones. God bless you forever.

Remembering you,

Emma

As time went by, Pablo got older and unable to travel. Since Emmaline (my daughter) lived in Texas, he never had a chance to see her baby (Gavin). Therefore, the only way Pablo could see the baby was in the pictures I sent to him. I honestly believe that when Pablo saw Gavin and Emmaline's pictures, he enjoyed one last moment of happiness.

"Patita" means small legs. We called him "The Patita Man" because he used to say my baby (Emmaline) had the cutest baby legs he had ever seen. Pablo had a great sense of humor. He loved to play with my baby and to help me care for her. Furthermore, Pablo not only helped me to take care of Emmaline as a baby, he also helped me to pay for her college tuition by giving me a check for five hundred dollars. These are only some of the things that demonstrate the one-of-a-kind man that he was.

Emmaline Is Born

I had been feeling symptoms of something happening to me for a few days. I had an idea of what it was but could not be sure. So I went to my doctor for a checkup. It didn't take the doctor too long to say, "Yes, you are having a baby—congratulations." I started to plan for another child. And since I had enjoyed Little Peter so much, I really didn't mind having another little boy. I told my husband when I got home, but he was not thrilled with the news. When I said to him, "I am pregnant," he looked at me and said, "So what do you want me to do?" And he walked away.

Time went by, and life went on relatively well. Peter Jr. and his friends, neighbors, and relatives were all waiting for the great day. It seemed to me that everyone in town was excited except my husband. But he was no problem; he was quiet most of the time. I was feeling fine as the day got closer. I went on maternity leave in October 1969.

Emmaline was born in November 1969. Fortunately, this time I didn't suffer as much physical pain as I did when Peter Jr. was born. I was feeling healthy and strong enough to face any kind of situation ahead of me. Peter Jr. was happy with his little sister and waiting impatiently to hold her in his arms. At night, he often took her from her crib to his bed to sleep with her. His friends came to the house to ask me, "Miss Gomez, can I hold the baby for a few minutes?" And I said, "As long as you bring her back to me." And they all held her for a few minutes. These boys were good; they all went to school and stayed away from trouble.

They loved my daughter, and they would not let anybody hold her without my permission. This was a group of five boys: four brothers—Pat, John, Michael, and Kevin—and Peter Jr., who was the leader. They all sat on the stoop with the baby waiting for their chance to hold her. Peter Jr. was always there making sure everything was okay. They were all in their teens, but unlike most teenagers today, they could be trusted. Emmaline grew up along with them, and to this day, they all remember and love her.

My sister Benedicta was not with me at the time. She was in nursing school in Puerto Rico. She came to see the baby for Christmas when Emmaline was only two months old. She fell in love with the baby, and she decided to continue her studies in New York. So she went back to Puerto Rico to do what had to be done before moving in with me. Soon after the holidays, she came back and attended school at night to complete her studies and to help me with the baby during the day.

Having my two children thirteen years apart was not my choice, but I do not regret it. God blessed me with a beautiful little girl who gave a new meaning to my life. I had been going through difficult times with my husband, feeling helpless and overwhelmed. I was afraid to make a bad decision, knowing that sooner rather than later, I would have to take some action to keep my sanity. With the birth of my daughter, I believed Peter could change his behavior. It was just wishful thinking on my part, because it never happened.

Peter kept making mistakes and never realized he was wrong. I remember that when I told him I was pregnant, he acted indifferent and unmoved, showing no interest in the matter. It seemed to me he did not care one way or the other. My feelings for him were slowly dissipating, and although he was aware of it, he did nothing about it. One more time, I knew I was facing a serious problem. Since the incident during our first Christmas and the situation after Little Peter's birth, I had been trying and hoping for a better relationship, but it did not happen. Instead of trying to make the situation better, Peter kept doing the things he knew upset me, like cursing and arguing with Little Peter. I could never tolerate cursing; it was something my parents made sure their children never learned.

Two of the many things Peter did knowing they disturbed me the most were swearing, especially in front of the kids, and talking about women while I was around. The cursing was to make me angry, and the talking was to make me jealous. I knew how hard he tried to make me jealous. Juan, a fellow from the church that we used to go, often came over after church just to chat with Peter. It didn't matter to them who was around, especially Emmaline.

Peter's behavior was pushing me over the edge, but with the new baby coming, I needed to stay in control. Once again, I had to set my priorities without losing faith and hope. I decided to let him do whatever made him happy, and disregard his nonsense for the sake of peace in the family. After all, Little Peter and his friends were excited about the new baby coming and were ready to help me care for her. He was no longer Little Peter; he had grown up to be a fine young man with a great sense of humor, and was now to be called Peter Jr.

Mother and daughter were happy and doing fine. Regardless of my problems with Peter, I was feeling strong and in control. As previously planned, my priority was my newborn baby. I wanted to make sure I gave her what she needed the most—good care and lots of love. Although Peter was not thrilled with the new baby, he was ready to help whenever he could. Unknown to me at the time, I was about to experience a big surprise, something that could end my worries and concerns. Like a blessing, my sister

Benedicta, who had been working as a practical nurse in Puerto Rico, decided to come to live with me to help me care for the baby and to continue her studies to become a registered nurse.

Emmaline grew up being loved and admired by neighbors and friends. She was my pride and joy. She made my life meaningful and worthy of all my struggles and emotional pain. With the birth of my baby and my sister's help, my life was rapidly turning around and everything seemed easier to handle. Amid the great responsibilities ahead of me, I always believed that everything was going to be all right. I felt confident that I was in the right direction to improve my quality of life and that soon I would see the light at the end of the tunnel.

Benedicta's help was a blessing unlike any other. She was a no-nonsense woman who meant what she said. I could not expect anything better than her unconditional help and love for my baby. Another unexpected surprise was one more visit from Pablo. He was also willing to help me care for the baby. He loved her like his own daughter and loved playing with her.

Everyone seemed happy except my husband. I was never able to figure him out. While he demonstrated so much love for Little Peter, he didn't show enough love for Emmaline. When he received his share of the brownstone house, he sent Little Peter $125.00—but nothing for Emmaline. Also, by order of the court, he had to send me for Emmaline's support $25.00; I don't remember if it was weekly or monthly, but he stopped doing it when she was still in high school. And there are many other examples of his ignorance.

My relationship with Peter had deteriorated to such an extent that for me, being with him was no longer a pleasure, but a sacrifice. For the sake of my children and until I was confident I could make it on my own, I could tolerate his childish behavior for some time longer. Since he was not violent and was likable and friendly,

I had no problem having him around. Besides, he was very helpful with the house chores and very well organized. Ironically, Peter was a good person but never learned to be a good husband nor a good father.

Cornell University and AFGE Local 2431

As previously mentioned, in February 1966, I was hired by the General Services Administration (GSA), a federal agency. After serving approximately fourteen months in a temporary status, I became a permanent employee and able to join the union. I do not recall accurately the year I joined the American Federation of Government Employees—AFGE—Local 2431, but I believe it was sometime in 1969. Thereafter I got involved in issues affecting workers and attended monthly meetings and other labor union events. Gene, the local president, had been searching for a treasurer for some time. But nobody was interested in that position. He spoke to me, but since I was going on maternity leave, I told him to see me after my return to duty.

I went on maternity leave from October 1969 to February 1970. I returned to work in February, when changes were being made within the agency. A temporary night shift was being implemented, and I was assigned as the night-shift supervisor. There were only seven or eight employees on night duty, most of them running the printing machines. They were not too happy having me as their supervisor, but everything went well. Once the changes and the reorganization ended, the night shift was terminated after only six months, and I went back to my bookbinder position during the day.

Meanwhile, due to the six months working at night and all the other activities and delays, I had not been able to contact Gene for a while. But I knew he had found Gladys, a longtime member, to help him.

Time went by, and we met during one of many meetings we both attended. He asked me to accept the treasurer position, and he explained it to me this way: "I've got good news for you; listen to me. I want you to attend some courses being offered by Cornell University Metropolitan Center in New York City." I quickly responded, "Cornell University? That's too expensive!" He said, "As an officer, the local would sponsor you through the Cornell University program." I said, "But officially I am not an officer." "That's what I need to explain to you. If you agree, everything should be fine." Gene continued saying, "Gladys does not want the position. She is just trying to help us. I would like you to talk to her." I knew Gladys very well, and I spoke to her. "I am willing to help you, but I do not want the position," Gladys told me.

I contacted Gene and said, "Gladys and I met and came to an agreement: I accepted, and she offered to help if needed." He was pleased and told me, "That's great; and since the Cornell program is about a year away, we have time to get ready." Gene explained the Cornell two-year program to me, and I was looking forward to being part of it. I don't remember the exact dates when some of these activities occurred, but I believe it was late in 1973, because the Cornell program ended in 1976.

Being a participant of this program was fascinating to me. It seemed as if it had been created on my behalf. The way in which it was designed offered me the greatest opportunity of my life. And as everything was taking place, my student life, though hectic and unexpected under the circumstances, was something to celebrate and admire. The Cornell University two-year program was coming to an end, but for me, it was a wake-up call.

After completing the program, if I continued toward a college degree, I would have twenty Cornell University college credits, transferable to the Empire State College's Center for Labor Studies in New York City. I realized all the work that would be involved, but I was ready for the challenge and ready to start. I was excited about going back to school. When I went to register, the university staff was friendly and helpful; they made me feel at home. I knew I was doing the right thing and had no doubt that I was going to do well. Nine years after I had attended an institute in Brooklyn to learn typing, I was following Pablo's advice: to go back to school and work toward a college degree.

Most of us understand the fact that nothing is perfect and try to adjust to it. Not so with my husband. Peter was never interested in what I was doing and never asked me about it. What I often heard from him was: "When is it over? For how much longer are you going to be doing that? I thought you had finished." He did not care about who did what, and much less about who was paying for my tuition. The only thing that perhaps could have made him happy was for me to stay home and have babies. I felt relaxed while in the classroom and when involved in other activities. It was comforting for me to know my two children, especially Emmaline, were well taken care of by my sister Benedicta. My children were what really mattered to me.

The first day in class, we introduced ourselves and told our own stories. The course was about working women, and obviously, all the students were women. To hear the women's stories was quite interesting. There were great similarities in our stories, and the women all seemed to enjoy listening and talking about the other students' stories. For example: "My husband is too demanding; he is hard to please," a woman said, this being seconded by most of them. Another example very similar to others was, "My husband always asks, 'why haven't you done what I asked you to do?' or 'Don't make me ask you again.'" Some of these women were not even allowed to leave the house without their husbands' permission. Others did not speak English and had to depend on their husbands practically for everything. It could make you wonder what goes on in some innocent people's everyday lives. And their stories explained why they were listening and learning from my story.

At that very moment, I was experiencing one of their main concerns, a demanding husband. I can tell you that my student life while at Cornell was hectic, but never out of control. If I had to do it all over again, I would not hesitate. It was while attending the courses at Cornell that I learned who I really was, which is in part, courageous for being able to kick obstacles out of my way and daring to attempt and do things most people do not dare to try.

At Cornell teachers were friendly and tried their best to make us feel comfortable and relaxed. I was excited to be back in school and confident that I would do well. I had no doubt that I was where I belonged—back in school. And then I was ready to continue my way to Empire State College to get what I deserved—a college degree. And I was ready to do so even if I had to kick Peter out of my way.

The Cornell University program was a two-year program designed and conveniently organized for adult students. Students earned one and a half college credits for each course satisfactorily completed. At the end of the program, all students with twenty college credits earned, received a certificate of completion. Students who continued their studies toward a college degree would be accepted along with their twenty college credits at Empire State College's Center for Labor Studies in New York City. I completed the program in 1976, with a high grade-point average. It was a great help and a perfect start for my academic development. Thereafter, I continued my studies toward a college degree. The AFGE Local 2431 financed my two-year program sponsored by Cornell University.

DIVORCE

I had met Peter in late 1949, my first year in high school and Peter's last year in junior high. We quickly developed a relationship, but we could not see each other as much as we would have liked to because the two schools were far apart. Regardless of the distance, we managed to keep our relationship going. We had no problem waiting for the next school year, when Peter would join me in high school.

When Peter started his first year of high school, our relationship got stronger. We were happy together and very much in love. Everything was going well, especially for me, being loved for the first time in my young life. As time went by, I noticed that Peter was paying more attention to me than to his schoolwork, and that did not make me happy. So I decided to help him do his homework before I went home. For me, schoolwork had priority over everything else, including our relationship. It was something that I had practiced from first grade on, and I was not about to give it up now. I was confident that we could continue our relationship without neglecting our schoolwork. For the next two years, we were happy doing the schoolwork together and enjoying our relationship.

I graduated from high school, and shortly thereafter, I left home for New York City. Peter graduated one year later, and as previously planned, he left home for New York City soon after as well. Once we were in New York, we got used to the new environment and to the different lifestyle. We loved each other and everything was going well. However, we were not aware about the difficult situation that we were soon going to experience. My mother could not accept our relationship, and it created serious problems between Peter and me. (Details on this topic have been explained previously.) Now I will bring to readers more incredible stories about my life.

Peter and I were no longer students, and we were slowly adjusting to the new environment and to our lives as young working adults. We enjoyed our relationship and doing the things we liked to do. But something unexpected that would change our lives forever was about to happen to us. We were young: Peter was twenty and I was twenty-one years old. Peter and I had been together for over four years, but getting married had never crossed our minds yet. As I mentioned earlier, my mother could not accept our relationship, and it had created a complicated and stressful situation for me. My relationship with Peter was rapidly deteriorating and I wanted to end it, but Peter refused. There was only one choice for me to make: to get married—and we did.

Most of my family loved Peter, and we were all happy about it. He was a very likable young man. Then on our first Christmas after the wedding, Peter made a big mistake. (Details previously explained.) From that day on, I was concerned about our future together. I began to take mental notes as he continued to make mistakes. It was difficult for me to comprehend the reason for his behavior, for it was evident that he loved me and I loved him as well. I never told my family and friends about my problems with Peter; I felt that it was better for me to let them believe that we were the perfect couple.

As time went by, I began to understand the reasons for his actions. Peter never thought that he could be wrong, even when he was told that he was. His next inexcusable mistake was when Little Peter was born. Though we were both excited about our beautiful baby, to him it made no difference. His actions were in total disregard for my feelings and my physical condition. Instead of demonstrating a sign of sympathy and consideration for my feelings and pains, he acted cold and indifferent. His actions were childish and selfish; they made me realize that a complicated and serious situation was in front of me and that I must take some action sooner rather than later.

We had been married for over three years, and there was no reason for his rude and hurtful behavior. After the first Christmas incident and his almost-cruel behavior after the baby was born, I was feeling confused and uncertain about our future. I had been doing a lot of thinking, but nothing seemed to me like the right thing to do. Peter loved the baby and took very good care of him. And now I had to think about our child more than about anything else. I could not afford to make a decision that could hurt our child. Little Peter meant everything to me, and he loved his father and enjoyed playing with him. Watching the two of them so happy together was all I needed to stop thinking about what to do and to decide what action to take.

Peter did not want me to continue my studies toward a college degree. He did not want me to go back to school after the completion of the two-year program at Cornell University, and he wanted me to end my union activities as well. He knew the Cornell program was ending. Several times he had asked me, "What are you going to do after the program ends; are you going to stay in school?" And I said, "Yes." Quickly he said, "What! Are you going to continue with your union activities also?" Again I said, "Yes." He got very upset and said, "You already have a husband, a job, a home, and two children; what else can you possibly want?" According to him, I had enough with what I had. Needless to say, we were having serious problems that were negatively affecting our married life. The situation had become difficult and complicated—almost impossible for me to endure. I knew that I would have to take some action to end the increasingly stressful situation that I had been experiencing for approximately fifteen years. But for the sake of our two children, I did not want to end our marriage. Besides my concern about our children, I was also worried about the effects of a divorce on my ambition for a college degree.

I had decided to continue my education, and I was not about to change my mind. So I met with Barbara Wertheimer (who is now deceased) to ask for her advice on perhaps the most difficult decision that I was to make in my entire life. Barbara was the director of the Trade Union Women's Studies program. She had also been a member of the faculty for the two-year program at Cornell University. Barbara had been advising me from the start of the program on how to cope with my personal problems without affecting my schoolwork and my role as a mother. We often met to talk about my situation at home. Her support meant a lot to me; it kept me focused on my work and confident that I would reach my goals. We developed a friendly and professional relationship that lasted even after the two-year program was over. We often talked about my personal problems, and she always made me feel good about myself. She was an inspirational woman who enjoyed helping her students to pursue their dreams.

Barbara often told me, "Emma, you are a strong woman. You seem to know how to handle very difficult situations when they come your way." In response, I said, "You might be right, Barbara, but sometimes it is very difficult and complicated." "I know so, but I also know that you can do it," she said. And I added, "I have to think about my children, myself, and my responsibilities, such as my home, my job, and my studies." Again Barbara said, "You can do it." I really did not know how to tell her about so many things in my life happening during the last fifteen years. We both had busy schedules and many interruptions. So, as she always said, "Let's meet again."

The next time we met, I told Barbara about my encounters with Peter. Although she knew about my situation at home, I had not mentioned to her my most difficult encounters with my husband. I said to her, "This is going to be difficult for you to believe, but it is true." Barbara just said, "Go on." I told her, "For approximately fifteen years, intimacy with my husband has been torture for me, rather than pleasure." She could not believe what I had just said. Then she said to me, "Tell me how you have tolerated such hurtful conditions for so long." I just told her, "It has been for the sake of my children and due to my insecurity about being able to make it on my own." Barbara was appalled with my incredible story. Then she added, "Only a courageous woman like you could cope so well as a mother and remain an excellent student while under such stressful conditions."

The most upsetting incident between Peter and me happened when he asked me to make a choice. We had been talking about my plans to continue my studies toward a bachelor's degree at Empire State College. Peter got very upset again and said, "I want you to make a choice: to stay in school and continue with your union activities, or to keep your husband." My response to him was, "I already made my choice: to stay in school and to continue with my union activities." He responded by saying, "Okay, I'm leaving." Then I said to him, "If you leave, don't ever come back."

After I finished my long story, Barbara asked me several personal questions, and she was not surprised with my answers. She asked me, "Are you sure what you have just said is what you want to do?" My answer was, "Absolutely." She then asked me, "Do you still love your husband? Do you think he deserves a second chance?" "Absolutely not," was my answer. I kept silent while listening to what she had to say. Barbara said, "After listening to you, I would advise you as if you were my own daughter." Barbara then said," There isn't too much more to be said—except for one thing, unfortunately: to end your marriage." And again, she offered me her support.

The divorce issue had been decided. Then Barbara and I talked about the impact of my decision on the children and myself. She made sure that I understood that her advice was just advice and not instructions as to what I must do. Only I could make the final decision on the matter. But she warned me that my actions must be final because changing my mind later would create an even more difficult situation for the children and me. I told Barbara that when I had made the choice that Peter asked me to make, I was convinced that it was the best thing for me to do and that there would be no turning back.

At the end of our meeting, as she always did, Barbara gave me friendly advice with her personal touch. She told me that based on the circumstances as I had explained them, I had made the right decision. And she added that against all odds, I would earn my college degree, and most certainly, improve the quality of my life. She said she admired me for my courage and my achievements, and for how well I had managed my responsibilities in an undesirable environment for fifteen years—as I had mentioned earlier. There is a lot more that I would like to tell readers about this unforgettable woman and about her contribution to my professional life.

For now I must go back to my own life story, for it is my reason for writing this book. But I still keep a letter from Barbara dated August 22, 1980, which is a pleasure to read, and I will include it in this book along with other illustrations. Barbara was my source of inspiration throughout the two-year program at Cornell University and thereafter, until lung cancer took her life at the too-young age of fifty-two. I want to remind readers that there were, and still are, beautiful people and things in this world that can make a difference in your life; Barbara's letter is one of them.

Barbara was not the only person who after listening to my story agreed with me that the best thing for me to do was to divorce Peter. Pablo, who had been staying in my house for some time, had been observing Peter's behavior. One day while I was working the night shift, Pablo called to tell me about an argument that was going on between Peter and Peter Jr., who was eighteen years old at the time. Pablo reported that father and son had been arguing for some time in the basement of the house. And he had heard Peter Jr. say to his father that one of them had to leave the house. Since his father would not leave, he said that he would. As Peter Jr. was about to walk out, Pablo told him to wait until he called me. He called and explained to me what had been going on between my husband and my son. Then he told me that there was no need for me to come home, that he had the situation under control and that Peter Jr. was not going anywhere.

The next day, since I was working the night shift, I asked Peter Jr. to tell me what had happened the day before. He told me exactly what Pablo had said to me, adding that if Pablo had not been there, no one could have guessed what would have happened. Some readers might wonder about Pablo's actions in my home. So let me tell you about this man. I am not trying to have you believe that Pablo was Mr. Perfect; such a person doesn't exist. Pablo had his own stories to tell. He was human, and humans are not perfect. What Pablo really was, without a doubt, was a very smart human being. Pablo lived in my house a significant portion of his life. Everyone in my neighborhood, and evidently in my home, loved, respected, and trusted him. He never expected favors or pay of any kind for whatever he did.

Pablo also told me that sometime later we would have to talk about the sensitive situation that I was facing. When we talked, he advised me to divorce my husband. Pablo had been trying to determine what could have been the reason for Peter's troublesome behavior. We had spoken about it several times. Thinking that Peter might be jealous of me because I had continued my education and he had not, Pablo had suggested to Peter that he also should go back to school. To our surprise, Peter agreed. Pablo went with him to a learning center in downtown Brooklyn, where he registered to attend a course in mathematics.

Peter purchased the textbook and other items required for the course. Then, after attending classes for the first week, he dropped out of the class. At this point, Pablo suggested to me that I not waste my time with Peter; he suggested I should continue my studies and divorce Peter. According to Pablo, it was the best thing to do for the sake of the children and for my own sake as well. He knew that Peter's habit of cursing was one of the main reasons for our frequent arguments. Furthermore, Peter often talked about me to others in a malicious and offensive manner. Peter Jr. could not stand the way his father spoke about me or tolerate his troublesome behavior any longer.

In July 1976, Peter returned to his parents' home in Yabucoa, Puerto Rico. After waiting one year in compliance with the law, he obtained an uncontested divorce from me and married a woman well-known to my sister Benedicta from her school days. I thought it was good for him to marry a good woman because, after all, he would always be my children's father. Soon after the divorce, he legally claimed his share of the brownstone house. Through his lawyer, he asked for thirty thousand dollars from me—and through my lawyer, he was granted twenty thousand. Ironically, this was an amount of money similar to the price of the house when we had purchased it. Peter asked for that amount of money from me in total disregard of his children and the other responsibilities he had left behind for me to deal with.

Peter knew I did not have any money available and therefore, I had to sell the house so he could get his share. By now, Peter Jr. was nineteen years old and had finished his first year of college. Emmaline was seven and in the second grade. But nothing mattered to Peter; according to him, my situation was not his problem. He just wanted his money at any cost to me.

FREDDY

Amid all the stories and hurtful events I endured, I had been lucky enough to find a new husband. I met Freddy in 1967, when he and two other employees, Ronny and Louis, came to work for GSA. Customarily new employees were introduced to all office employees. So I was asked to introduce the three new ones.

At the time, the GSA office was located at 30 Church Street in Manhattan, the original World Trade Center site. That day, I accompanied the new employees to lunch. Thereafter, Louis and Ronny went their own ways. Freddy chose to keep me company at lunchtime, especially when he had no money to pay for his own lunch. During breaks Freddy often sat by me. Sometimes he seemed unhappy and moody, but we became friends anyway. The three of them often visited me and enjoyed summer in my backyard with my family, including Peter. Freddy was quiet but friendly. We used to talk about our life experiences and our families. We both had stories to tell, although of a different nature. Freddy had voluntarily joined the US Marine Corps at age seventeen, serving from 1957 through 1963 and receiving an honorable discharge.

Freddy had not been as lucky as I was when I was young. He never had that special person to show him the road to success. I had several of those special people who guided me through my success. And I feel great satisfaction for sharing my wisdom with Freddy, and especially making a difference and improving his quality of life. Today he can look at the beginning and at the end of his thirty-year career with the New York City Transit Authority, going from bus driver to superintendent of revenue collection. If that is not a remarkable achievement, what is?

In the meantime, I had found out that I was pregnant. The next morning I told everybody in the office, and they were happy for me. However, Freddy did not like Bill, the man running the machine near him. So Bill started a rumor that my baby was Freddy's. But all he could do was to wait until the baby was born. According to Bill, if the baby was white, it was Peter's; if it was dark, it was Freddy's. Exactly one month after Emmaline's birth, I took her to the office. She was white and beautiful. Once Bill saw the baby, all he could say was, "No, that can't be Freddy's baby. It is her husband's." But the damage had already been done; Freddy remained moody and disturbed. Months later he quietly left GSA and went to work for the New York City Transit Authority as a bus driver. Freddy didn't even say good-bye to me, and I did not see him again for five years.

Ironically, one day as I was sitting by the kitchen table reading, Peter walked in and said, "Look what I found." And Freddy walked in. I asked him, "What are you doing around here?" He said, "I'm driving the 75." That is the bus line passing by my house. Peter left us in the kitchen and sat in the living room watching TV. Then I asked Freddy, "How long have you been driving the 75?" He answered, "For seven years." And I said, "Wow, that's a long time." Then we spoke for a while longer before he left.

Freddy said good night to Peter and me, and asked us if he could come by some other time. We said yes and he left. Once he came by and I was not home, but Peter was. He asked Peter, "Where is Emma?" Peter said, "She is in the Catskill Mountains for the weekend." Another day while I was walking down the block, he passed me by while driving the bus, and we waved at each other. That day after work, he stopped by and I was not home, but Peter was. He asked Peter again, "Where is Emma?" Peter responded,

"She is in the hospital." "But I saw her walking down the block this morning. What is wrong with her?" Freddy asked. And Peter said, "She is having a small surgery on her breast." Freddy did not know what to believe, but he was convinced something was happening between Peter and me. Then he asked Peter, "Are you going to see her?" Peter responded, "No, but if you want to see her, she is in room #----."

Freddy went to visit and brought me a strawberry shake. He remembered that was what I had for lunch years back when we had lunch together. He talked to the two ladies in the room with me while I drank my shake. After he left the room, they said to me, "What a sweet husband you have! He knows what you like—strawberry shakes."

During the unexpected meeting in my house, Freddy had asked me, "What have you been doing since the last time we saw each other?" I told him, "I am going to school." He then said, "What school?" And I told him, "Cornell University on East Forty-Third Street." Then, one day after class as I was leaving the building, he was waiting for me. He carried my books as we walked from east to west to take the train to Brooklyn. It was a long walk, so Freddy asked me, "Do you walk all this at night by yourself?" "I have no choice," I said. "I will come for you on my days off," he said, and he did. Peter had no idea where I was or what I was doing. He never asked me, though at times he implied that I was with someone else. But he did not mean I was with Freddy. Peter never suspected anything was going on between Freddy and me.

I can understand that some people might see my meetings with Freddy as romantic encounters, but they were not. We were just not ready to face another complicated situation. Although our issues were of a different nature, they were of utmost importance to us.

Freddy had been a bus driver in Brooklyn for over seven years and had created a chronic sick-leave abuse record. He had repetitiously exceeded the number of sick days allowed per employee. And if continued, he would lose any chance for promotion and his job as well. He had to make some changes for the sake of saving his job. And he needed a source of support and advice. Somehow Freddy was able to turn himself around and believe in himself. Perhaps by watching me handling my struggles and listening to my advice, he saw the light at the end of the tunnel.

On the long July Fourth weekend in 1976, Freddy saw Peter walking up the block with an extra-large suitcase. He called Peter's attention and he let him on the bus. Peter said, "Hello." Freddy said, "Where are you going?" Peter responded, "To Puerto Rico." Freddy said, "Are you putting Emma in that suitcase? It's big enough." Peter quickly answered, "No, I'm leaving her. Do you want her? You can have that -----" (not a good word). I don't know what Freddy said, but I think it was nothing.

The next day, Peter went back home to Puerto Rico. I did not see him again until I visited Puerto Rico in 1995. And this is what happened: I was in a store with Benedicta, and Peter walked in. He looked at me and said, "Como estas?" (How are you?) He quickly gave me a kiss on the cheek and left without saying anything else. People say, "Go figure." And I add, "If you can, because I can't."

As for Freddy, "one man's loss is another man's gain." He did just what Peter told him to do. He married me in April 1978. There was no engagement, no contemporary romance, and no big wedding celebration. We were married by Judge Darling, a Catskill Mountains judge. We had a small celebration in my sister Margaret's summer house, also in the Catskills. Everyone had a great time, including Mother, who was present at this wedding.

 **REGION TWO REVIEW**

FALL 1981

Emma Gomez:
Displaying 'true grit,' she wins her college degree

The very thought of it might have shocked many of us. But anyone who handles a nightly commute on New York's subways (missing only one class in seven years) isn't about to be daunted by the prospect of delivering a commencement address to 1200 people at the Waldorf-Astoria.

That's the story on Emma Gomez, a wife and a mother who was chosen as student speaker (valedictorian) for this year's program of the Empire State College, Center for Labor Studies and adult-oriented affiliate of the State University of New York.

Where did a 16-year veteran of GSA (currently an FSS Supply Clerk) get the idea, the drive and the time

to spend those many nights commuting between Brooklyn and Manhattan's Times Square in pursuit of a B.A. in Labor Studies?

Well, it all began with a single non-credit course, an outgrowth of her interest in the labor movement and in women's rights.

The commencement at the Waldorf-Astoria involved 325 graduates, largest in the institution's 10-year history.

And speaking of role models, Emma wasn't just No. 1; she also happened to be the first woman and only Hispanic person to achieve this distinction.

The region's most recent (and perhaps most unusual) college grad began her GSA career in Printing and Distribution. Four years ago she moved to FSS Requisition & Control, in a job which entails paperwork and some research and customer contact.

She's also active elsewhere in GSA as an EEO counselor and as a member and Vice-Chairperson of the Hispanic Employment Program (see photo).

As an expert in guiding non-English speaking workers through the intricacies of basic English, Gomez has instructed classes sponsored by the Cornell University Women's Studies Program, also based in midtown Manhattan. In addition, she has been a volunteer teacher of special classes for Local 169 of the Amalgamated Clothing and Textile Workers Union.

Not bad at all for someone who had no idea that any of this would happen when she finished high school 28 years ago.

Richard Majica and Emma Gomez are Chairperson and Vice chairperson, respectively, of the region's active Hispanic Employment Committee. See Emma's story above.

GSA article – This article was written by an employee of the GSA Business Services Center in 1981.

Volunteer Profile

Emma Gomez has spent most of her life helping people and working to improve the world around her. At one time, Emma was an active member of 15 different organizations. She was a labor union officer, a teacher of English as a Second Language and she attended the historic National Women's Conference in 1979, at the height of the women's rights movement. For the past seven years, Emma has turned her amazing energies toward volunteering in Prospect Park. "The Park has been my friend for many years," she says. And she is a friend to the Park in countless ways. She has done everything from leading Trolley tours to staffing the Celebrate Brooklyn! Festival to planting flowers. She's even taught Alliance staff members the fine art of weaving.

"The hours I spend here are so precious to me. The people are so nice and I get to admire nature and see shows. It's good therapy," she says. She also realizes how important the Park is to the people of New York City. "Every time I am in the Park, people seem happy to be here. These days, people don't like to travel as much and the Park is close by, safe and free for all to enjoy." Emma espouses the belief that, "everybody needs somebody." We are extremely grateful to be one of the beneficiaries of her caring philosophy. Call (718) 965-8960 to volunteer in the Park. It's fun and it works!

Volunteer profile – I did volunteer work
in Prospect Park for seven years.

My parents.

Sister Benedicta - who has been more than a sister to me.

Brother Nick.

Brother Fausto.

My family in 1939 - Except Brother Fausto who was
unavailable at the time. From left to right: Juanita, Nick,
Mother, (expecting Sister Benedicta), Father, holding Baby
Margaret, and me (trying to hide my barefoot feet), Sister
Mary, and Sister Rose. Sister Sylvia had not been born yet.

My wedding.

Mother and seven daughters.

A Darling Little Girl

She is sweet and very gracious
She is beautiful and petite
She has talent and style
With a charm that is unique.

She wears big brown eyes
To match her long brown hair
And her angel-like smile
Sends a message through the air.

No words can just explain
The expression on her face
It is that of love and affection
With such a heavenly grace.

Emmaline her name is
With the silhouette of a dream
As radiant as a sunflower…
What else can a little girl be?

I wrote this poem about my daughter as part of a school project.

My son Peter and his wife Sonia.

Emmaline and Aaron on their wedding day.

Copy of a beautiful letter by Emmaline.

Emma Gomez

August 11, 1986

Dear Mom and Dad:

I want to tell you how happy I am and how fortunate I consider myself for having you as my parents. I know words cannot express the feeling in me at the time, but I will try to communicate it to you somehow.

You have given me the greatest thrill of my life by making it possible for me to be a participant in the Miss-Metro New York National Teen-Ager Pageant. To many girls of my age an event like this is only a dream; thanks to you, Mom and Dad, mine is a reality!

Being a participant in this pageant means so much to me, for the activities and responsibilities involved offer me an opportunity to prepare myself to enjoy a more meaningful life in the future.

The pageant will be an unforgettable experience for me because on its first night I celebrate my 17th birthday. And what a birthday gift that is…to be sponsored by my parents!!!

Mom and Dad, even if I don't win the crown I am still a winner, for I have you as my parents. But most of all, I am so proud to be your daughter and most certain that you are so proud to be my parents.

Thank you Mom…Thank you Dad…

With all my love,

Your Em

Picture of the Latin- Women- to- China- Group in 1981. In the background is a picture of Mao-Tse-Tung's birth-place, which is now a museum. I am the first one sitting in the front row, on the left.

My summer home - Sister Benedicta and I owned this house in the New York State Catskill Mountains for twenty years.

Dinner Dance Event honoring me and other union officers on December 2, 1978 at the Statler Hilton Hotel in New York City. From the left: Margaret (sitting), her husband Pablo, Harry (friend), Sylvia, me, Benedicta, and my husband Freddy.

American Federation of Government
Employees (AFGE) convention in Boston 1974,
Local-2431. President Gene, and me.

On the roof – Here I am on the roof of the Federal Plaza
Building, (lower right hand corner) while materials
for the up-grading of the building's heating and air
conditioning systems were being dropped-off via helicopter.
This was an interesting learning experience for me

August 22, 1980

Dear Emma;

I have meant to write you for the longest time, life has been
so very hectic. It still is, but I feel that I just must thank you
for your thoughtfulness and kindness. I am thrilled and honored
to have a copy of your beautiful, wonderful report on your trip
to China. When I have finished with it, as you know, it will be
given to the Library on Working Women, where it will be cata-
logued and placed on the shelf with the other reference books
in the Women's Collection. I am impressed not only with your
thoroughness and the comprehensive nature of the report, but with
its imaginativeness as well, with the way you put it together. It
is an excellent piece of work.

I appreciate the scarves, and love and cherish them because you
brought them back personally for me. And the story of the clock
is one that I can never forget. Each time I travel, and use the
clock you gave me, you will be there with me in the room. In a
way, you'll be keeping me company --- so how can I ever be lonely
on my journeys?? But it will take me some time to get over feeling guilty because you spent so much effort and energy on replacing
the clock. I do thank you from the bottom of my heart.

I am so glad you had such a marvelous time on the trip and that
it meant so much to you. It is another world, China is, and one
that seems elusive once we have been back for a while. But an
unforgettable experience and certainly we come back somewhat
different people from what we were when we left.

My warmest to you and your husband, and again my deepest thanks.

In sisterhood,

Barbara Wertheimer

Barbara's letter, as mentioned in the chapter, My Trip to China.

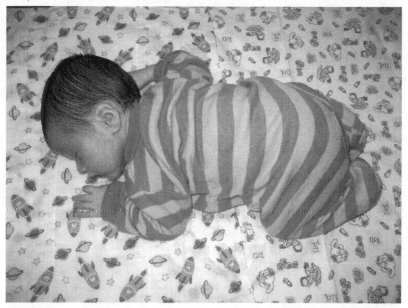

My favorite picture - My grandson Gavin three months old.

Gavin's first birthday.

Gavin at age six.

EMPIRE STATE COLLEGE'S CENTER FOR LABOR STUDIES

In September 1976, I entered the Empire State College's Center for Labor Studies in New York City, pursuing a college degree. Though I was excited about being able to further my education, I was also nervous to be in the new college environment. In my first course, Work and Contemporary Social Issues, almost all the students were men, and I was the only Hispanic.

My jitters and uneasy feelings at the start of my first year at Empire State College soon disappeared. I had no problems participating in the course activities or being the only woman and only Hispanic in the class. To my surprise, I quickly became one of the most outspoken students and the most recognized by teachers and classmates. Right from the start, I knew that all the struggles and sacrifices I had previously experienced had been my learning tools. And I could not keep myself from often thinking about the people, the events, and the things in my life that I believed had been responsible for getting me to where I was at that moment—in a classroom, furthering my education.

When I think about my life in retrospect, I say to myself that by knowing great educators such as Pablo and Barbara, indeed I have been a lucky person. They were not only highly educated people; they were also everyday people who enjoyed sharing their wisdom with other human beings like me. I also consider myself lucky for having parents who, with limited education, did a commendable job of teaching me well. They set me on the road to a meaningful and successful future. There is a reason for everything, and I believe the reason for my unprecedented successes were the lessons learned from my parents during my childhood and the way in which they raised me.

Before I entered Cornell University and Empire State College, I had doubts about my future. I could not imagine what kind of performance I could achieve by going back to school after having being out of a school environment for twenty years. Besides being a Hispanic woman, there were other factors that created doubt and uncertainty on how well I would perform in the classroom. I was concerned about being a housewife, being a mother, having a full-time job, and having disagreements with my husband. Nonetheless, after listening to the great educators of these learning institutions and with the support of Barbara and Pablo, I became convinced that I would be the brilliant student that I had been in the past.

The faculty at Cornell and Empire State did not hesitate to expect the best from me. I did not have to ask for their help or their support; I got it without asking, even though they did not know me. As I went from one classroom to another, I experienced a happy and relaxed environment, which made a difference in the classroom setting. The mentors were friendly and often made positive comments about their students. The students felt free to ask the professors for help with their classwork whenever needed. I enjoyed the mentors' friendly teaching methods, for it made learning much easier. Time went by, and I kept getting more involved in regular class events and activities. I felt so happy being in such a great environment, where students and teachers felt like family and we could learn from each other. It was evident that the teachers knew what they were there for and that they did it extremely well. I felt relaxed and confident that I would keep doing well in school. This feeling of confidence helped me not to think about my problems with my husband and the difficult situation that I had been enduring for so long.

As is a common procedure in learning institutions, at the end of each course, students received their marks, or their evaluations, from their mentors. My evaluations, in each one of my mentors' words, were like excerpts from my life story. All of the mentors, teachers, and supervisors who at one time or another in my life taught or advised me on anything had evaluated me as superior. I would like to share some statements made by my professors in my evaluations while I was attending Cornell and Empire State. The following is a quote from Mentor Ward, in the course Adult Development at Empire State College in 1980: "Ms. Gomez summarized the readings and also analyzed each approach and applied it to her own life or to the world she has observed." Statements like this have been made throughout my life. I hope that reading statements like them could benefit readers by helping them to clearly understand the point I am trying to make and the message I'd like to convey to them as they read my book. There are other interesting statements from my mentors' evaluations while I was attending these great learning institutions.

Professor Kelber was another person who had great influence in my academic and professional life. This man was one of the finest human beings I have ever known. His struggles, his achievements, and his sacrifices for the benefit of working people were beyond comparison. Although approaching the age of ninety-eight, he was still going strong in his labor union activities on behalf of working people. I consider myself very fortunate for having been one of his students in three different courses at Empire State. His evaluations of my schoolwork are so inspiring and meaningful that it's a pleasure reading them. Readers can also benefit by reading Professor Kelber's words on human behavior. Human behavior is difficult to explain. We all behave in different ways, and almost always, we believe our way is the right way, though it might not be so. I believe human behavior is a powerful ingredient in everything we say and do every single day of our lives.

In 1977, I attended the course Principles of Human Behavior with Professor Kelber as my mentor. The following is an excerpt from my evaluation by him: "I felt that the interchange of views and experiences with other students helped her in the analysis of her own life." Once again, it was a statement relevant to my life story. I believe what Professor Kelber said is true because I have done it many times in my life: you are most likely to learn something when you listen to other people's opinions and advice. In Professor Kelber's own words, "When we pay attention to what others are saying, chances are we learn something." He always advised his students to, in his own words, "Be cautious when you speak because you never know who might be listening." I believe this is true because sometimes we say things that unintentionally can offend someone. If I resent something you said, I might not even need to say anything; my behavior would speak for me.

Another course I attended with Professor Kelber as my mentor was China and US Foreign Policy," in 1980. This was the last course I needed to complete my requirements for the bachelor's degree. And what a wonderful learning experience it was! An experience like this is more like a dream than reality. My assignment for the entire trimester (the school year was divided in three-month periods instead of semesters) was to make a monthlong trip to China, consisting of two parts: (1) a study of the status of women in China and (2) American foreign policy. An excerpt from my final evaluation by Professor Kelber is as follows: "I am persuaded that Ms. Gomez has completed the requirements of this contract on an exceptionally high performance level. I recommend that she be granted nine credits for this three-quarter-time contract."

I'd like to invite readers to read one more excerpt from my evaluation by another mentor, Professor Lynch, for the course Effective Communication II. This mentor was great; the students could not get away with any error made in the classroom. He was tough and strict with the students, and he was there to teach us and we were there to listen to him and to learn our lessons. He often told us that a person who can accept criticism is a smart person. And he loved to apply his philosophy on us, his students. Though some students did not care for his teaching methods, they couldn't deny that in fact, they were learning their lessons. In the following excerpt from my evaluation, Professor Lynch demonstrated what he expected from his students and the message he wanted to convey to us: "I admired Emma Gomez's attention to her work and professional attitude. She is intelligent, forthright, and reliable. I particularly appreciated her attitude of acceptance when one of her themes was chosen to demonstrate how a fellow student's theme on the same topic was, in the mentor's opinion, better written. She accepted criticism well and understood that her being the 'guinea pig' was for the benefit of all. She is chipper, humorous, and humane—these personal qualities contributed to the feeling of well-being in the classroom setting."

I think the point that Professor Lynch was trying to make in my evaluation was similar to what I am trying to convey to readers in my book. If you make a mistake, accept it, learn from it, and move on. It is wise to accept criticism; it might prevent you from making similar mistakes in the future. Professor Lynch also expressed admiration for my punctuality and reliability. He acknowledged the fact that during the seven-year period that I attended school, I was absent from class only once. The reason for the absence was that I had been nominated as a candidate for officer in AFGE Local 2431. And in compliance with union rules, I had to be present to be elected. According to Professor Lynch, my superior attendance and my election as a union officer had been a remarkable and commendable achievement for me.

I had previously served unofficially as treasurer and as secretary-treasurer for the local. But I had never been officially elected.

Graduation time was approaching, and the seven years of traveling at night on the New York City subways to attend classes after finishing work at my full-time job were coming to an end. Although seven years might sound like a long time, to me it did not seem that long. I had been able to shorten my schooltime by one full year. For a part-time student, it normally takes eight years to complete the requirements for a bachelor's degree. I advanced one year by taking several tests based on my lifetime college-level activities, including my employment. I did so well in all the tests that I was granted enough college credits to skip two trimesters. I do not remember the number of credits I was given for my life experience, but I believe it was eight or nine. With my trip to China, for which I was awarded nine credits, I earned the additional credits needed to complete my degree.

My going-back-to-school experience was unforgettable for me for many reasons. It was something I had never expected or even thought about. I never could have imagined some of the events that took place toward the end of the seven years that I was back in school. For example, one day while I was at work after my return from China, Professor Kelber called to tell me that I had completed all the requirements for my bachelor's degree. With my trip to China, I had earned nine credits, and that was all I needed to complete the requirements for the degree. Therefore, there was no need for me to do anything else at that time. I just had to wait for graduation day, which I would be contacted about in advance. I do not remember what I said to Professor Kelber; I just wanted to make sure that I was not dreaming. I thought that this kind of phone call could only happen in the movies or in dreams. I knew my report had been well prepared and comprehensive, but since that was my style, it didn't feel that extraordinary. For a moment, I looked outside my office window in disbelief. I said to myself, this was a once-in-a-lifetime call; nothing better than this could happen to me ever again—but another surreal phone call was to come my way yet again.

I had received Professor Kelber's call in late 1979. Then in the early spring of 1980 while at work, I received a call from a classmate. I believe her name was Ruth. She gave me another once-in-a-lifetime call. What Ruth told me certainly made my heart skip a beat: I had been selected by students and faculty to be the valedictorian of Empire State College's Center for Labor Studies' 1980 graduating class. This call left me speechless. Both calls had been made during the school year's last trimester. Since I was not required to attend class at the time because I had already completed the requirements for my degree, I had to contain my excitement until I got home. Telling my coworkers would not have done any good, but there was one lady, Gladys, who was very happy for me and always wished me the best.

Before graduation day, I received several calls from the graduation committee. They wanted to let me know what I had to do for my big day and how to prepare myself to deliver the graduating class speech on behalf of the graduates. I was to write a ten-minute speech, and if I needed help writing it, I could call Professor Semel. She had been my speech-writing mentor at Cornell. At this point, I felt that I needed help on everything. Obviously, I was under a lot of pressure and feeling stressed out. Though all these events were of great significance for me, I was unprepared for them because I never expected something like this to happen to me. I called Professor Semel and told her I was overwhelmed, with so much going on for me all at once, and that I needed help writing my speech.

I should have known Professor Semel's response without even asking for her help. She told me that she had no doubt I could do it all by myself. However, she would be there to give me her support and guidance—and her help if needed. As for my feeling stressed out, she said not to worry, that it was human nature. She told me to relax and think about what I wanted to say in the speech and not to rush it because there was still some time before the date of the event. She advised me to write the speech at home and then bring it to her for her review. I did what she told me to do, and when I went to see her, she was fascinated with the work I had done writing the speech. There was hardly anything to be added or changed in it. She said she had always been proud to have me as her student, and according to her, my speech was very well written. Now that my speech had been taken care of, I felt that perhaps I could relax a bit without so much pressure on me.

In the meantime, I had been talking with Professor Lynch, who I have mentioned earlier was my mentor for the Effective Communication II course. He had advised me about certain incidents that could happen to anyone while giving a speech. For example, he said if you forget a line or change a word, just continue speaking without trying to clarify anything. In his opinion, people wouldn't even notice such a minor incident because either they had not been listening or they had been just looking at me. He also told me that being nervous was a natural feeling for anyone speaking in front of an audience. Professor Lynch made me feel confident that I would do well. And he would be seating in the front row right in front of me.

Some members of my family and friends were there for me. They were there offering me their support and were even more nervous than me, especially my husband Freddy. Besides Freddy, three of my sisters were there: Margaret and her husband, Pablo, Benedicta, and Sylvia. My friend Harry Rodriguez, now a retired professor, who offered me his help and support throughout my college years, was also there.

Graduation day arrived, but this was not a traditional graduation. It was a unique event for several reasons: 1) It was being held at the Waldorf Astoria Hotel, one of the best recognized and well-known hotels in New York City. 2) This was the largest graduating class in the history of the Labor College (as it is commonly called). 3) The first group of the Electrical Workers Union Local 3 was graduating. 4) It was the tenth anniversary of the founding of the

Center for Labor Studies. Besides all of the above, I was the first female and the first Hispanic ever to represent a graduating class of the Empire State College's Center for Labor Studies. Evidently, there were enough reasons for a great celebration, and it was so. However, years later, some friends and relatives told me that, in their opinion, I had not been given the recognition I deserved. My achievements had been history-making, but practically unnoticed.

Some of the topics cited above were included in my speech. But the most unforgettable incident for me was what I said as I read the first line of the speech. I meant to say: It is with great *pleasure* that I speak to you. Instead I said, "It is with great *pressure* that I speak to you." Though by changing the word I was indirectly telling the truth, it was not what I was supposed to say. At the end of the event, I realized that Professor Lynch had been right. Since no one mentioned anything to me after the speech, I wondered if anyone had been listening or if they had just been looking at me—including Professor Lynch. Everybody was congratulating me without saying anything about *pleasure* or *pressure*. So I just had to believe that rather than listening, they were looking at me in disbelief, perhaps wondering how I got there. I would like readers to keep in mind the best and last lines from my speech. I said: "It was not easy; at times I stumbled, but somehow I managed not to fall." I do believe that your future can be as successful as you want it to be if you work hard enough to make it be—as I did.

My Trip to China

I would like to chronicle the details of my trip to China, which was one of the most interesting and talked-about experiences of my life. This was, and still is, an event that I will never forget. As a learning experience, it went above and beyond its purpose and expectations. It has been used as a learning tool by children, and adults as well.

We were a group of fourteen Latin workingwomen from the United States, representing various occupations and activities. There were industrial workers, trade unionists, social workers, educators, students, community activists, and political activists. Individually, each person had her own specific purpose for going. The trip had been methodically organized, and it required some basic knowledge about China's political and social issues. As assigned by my mentor, Professor Kelber, my specific purpose for the trip consisted of two parts: (1) I was to make a study of the status of women in China and then write a substantial report on my experiences with and observations about Chinese women. I also had to read several books on China. (2) The second part of my assignment had to do with American foreign policy. For this part, I was assigned reading about the Indo-China refugee problem and US foreign policy with regard to Iran, the United Nations, and others. Besides our individual assignments, in order to be ready for the trip, we attended several training sessions, which had been prepared by the leader of the expedition.

I do not recall how this trip originated or how I got to be part of it. I was not aware that recruitment for women to be part of the group was going on until I was asked to be part of it. Though I had no idea what the trip was about, it seemed like a once-in-a-lifetime opportunity for me to experience life in a foreign country, so I joined the group. I believe it was one of my mentors who contacted me about having been chosen to go and who also informed me about what to do next. Once the group was organized, we elected Carmen as our leader. We were told to let Carmen know how many of us could not afford the expense of the trip, which was twelve hundred dollars. Those of us who did not have the money could have fund-raising activities, as a group or individually. We decided to go both ways and to help each other, and we did. We were able to collect enough money to help those who were short. We were also instructed to get a passport and that each one of us had to provide a small biography, obviously with some personal information. Due to the fact that the People's Republic of China was a communist country, we had to notify our government about the nature of our trip and who was going, so we did.

After getting the go-ahead from our government, we had several meetings to prepare us for the trip. We learned some basic words in Chinese such as: my name is …, thank you, and other necessary phrases. We were asked to bring the money for the airline fare to Carmen, so she could purchase the tickets for us. She advised us to follow our tour guides' instructions. This was important because at the time, the United States and China had not yet restored communication and friendship with each other. Therefore, with China being a communist country, we were going to be closely watched and followed by the Chinese government. Although we all felt nervous because we were going so far from home for the first time in our lives, we were looking forward to the trip. The day before departure, the group met for the last time to make sure we were ready for our journey to the unknown—and ready we were.

We were to depart on Tuesday, April 1, 1980. Ironically, on this day, New York City was affected by a transit strike that began in the early morning hours. Consequently, fearing delays on the road, I left home with ample time to get to the airport early enough to meet the girls and be on time for the flight. Everyone else was nervous about getting there too, and so they also arrived early. And since we knew that it was going to be a long trip, we had a good breakfast at the airport.

We departed from Kennedy Airport at 12:10 p.m. via Japan Airlines, and arrived at Anchorage Airport, Alaska, at 2:00 p.m. After a short stop in Alaska, we departed for Narita Airport, Tokyo, and arrived at 6:15 p.m. (4:15 a.m. New York time). We took a short rest before boarding a new flight to Hong Kong and arrived there at 7:25 p.m. Needless to say, we were tired and sleepy after traveling for so many hours. At the airport, we met our tour guide, who drove us by bus to the Plaza Hotel, where we spent the next two days.

The next day, after breakfast, I went shopping for souvenirs with Olympia, one of the girls in the group. And to my surprise, I experienced an unexpected incident, something unlikely to happen to a tourist. Olympia was looking at an expensive handbag, and she called me over and asked for my opinion on the price. I quietly indicated to her that she could find the same bag at home at a lower price. She said I was right and did not purchase the bag. I had placed my jacket on the counter while I paid for some items I had chosen, and I walked out without my jacket. A bit later, I went back for it and asked the man at the counter if he had seen my jacket. He responded in a very sarcastic manner, telling me to go back home, where I could purchase the same bag at a lower price. Olympia had noticed the man had been watching us and evidently he had heard what I said.

In previous chapters, I mentioned that I would let readers know more details of my stories as I continued my book. So now, I will explain another unexpected incident that happened to me during my trip to China. It was the reason for Barbara's meaningful and moving letter to me after I returned from the trip. Her letter is one of the illustrations I have included in my book because it is like a picture of the remarkable and unforgettable human being that Barbara was. In her letter, Barbara mentioned a clock and some scarves. I purchased these two scarves from a street vendor. They were of different colors and Chinese designs, something I knew Barbara liked. They were my gift for her. But the clock had a heartbreaking story behind it, which I painfully endured and will never forget.

Barbara and her husband were professionals who often traveled (not always together) as part of their jobs. Though her husband had passed a few years earlier, she often mentioned him to me. When she was told that I had been chosen to be part of the Latin-Women-to-China group, she was excited and happy for me. One day, Barbara called me to go to her office because she had something for me. When I got there she told me, "I want you to be well prepared for your trip. So it is very important for you to bring an alarm clock with you; without it, you might not get up on time, causing delays in daily activities." Then she looked in her pocketbook and took out a small box. Barbara held the small box with one hand and covered it with her other hand, as if holding something of a special meaning for her—and it was. She opened the little box and showed me the clock. What she told me about the clock brought tears to my eyes. She said, "My husband always took this clock with him when he traveled. And just before he died, he gave it to me. He told me to bring it with me whenever I travel, and he will always be with me."

Barbara continued to say beautiful things about me and about her husband and the clock, which made me wonder if I should take the clock with me. She said, "This clock means so much to me; it is my treasure." I was moved by her words, especially when she said, "But you are like a daughter to me." I did not know what to say. And I just said, "Barbara, you make me feel proud and so lucky I know you." A bit concerned, I took the clock with me. My concern was justified, to say the least; the clock disappeared from my hotel room in Nanking. I contacted the hotel management several times, but it did not matter to them. All they said to me was that they would look for it the next day, and that if it was found, they would contact me. I knew the clock was gone, and all I could do was to face reality. However, coming home without Barbara's clock was not a reality I wanted to face. Obviously, it was going to be difficult and painful for me to confess that I had lost her "treasure."

My trip to China in April 1980 took place at a time when the United States and China were trying to improve their diplomatic relations. They were also trying to restore communication and friendship between the two countries. Evidently it was not the right time for a group of American minority women to visit China. Nevertheless, regardless of the incidents and other inconveniences experienced, we accomplished our goals with great success. When President Nixon visited the People's Republic of China in February 1972, he called his trip, "The week that changed the world."

I called mine, "The once-in-a-lifetime learning experience."

When I returned home, I had to decide what to do about Barbara's lost clock. My sister Benedicta and I had been talking about buying her a new one, though I knew I would not find a similar one at any store, regardless of the price. Nonetheless, we went into Manhattan in search of a clock. We visited all the stores in sight but found nothing like what we were looking for. Finally, I bought one that was not particularly similar but was attractive and the same size as the lost one. The next day I went to see Barbara at her home in Manhattan. I had contacted her earlier to let her know I was going to see her. I did not mention anything about the clock when I called; I just told her that I had a story to tell her. As she opened the door to let me in, she noticed that I did not appear happy. I do not remember what I said first, but when I told her that I had lost her clock, she came closer to me and said, "Don't worry, honey, that was a material thing. What is important is that you are back home safe."

Barbara continued talking and trying to change my mood. When I gave her the new clock and the scarves, she got excited and a bit emotional. Then she told me that I did not have to buy her a new clock because she understood that sometimes things happen that are beyond our control. While holding the new clock in her hands, Barbara said that from that time on, whenever she traveled, she would bring the clock with her and she would never be alone because I would be there with her. Days later, I received my beautiful letter from Barbara, dated August 22, 1980. And just as I mentioned earlier, I have included this letter in my book as an illustration, hoping the readers can enjoy reading it, for it is worthy of reading.

As I mentioned earlier, Professor Kelber granted me nine college credits for my written reports on my trip to China. I also mentioned that children, as well as adults, benefited somehow by my reports on the trip. After my trip to China, I wrote a comprehensive report, without leaving out any details, on what I had learned and observed, as well as on my unexpected experiences. Besides the written report, I had kept a journal, citing all my actions and activities from the day I left my home until the day I returned. The title for my report and the journal was "The China Experience, 1980." But the most interesting part of my work during this trip was the exhibit I prepared, with illustrations depicting the different activities and places visited by the group. One thing that I enjoyed the most was meeting the Chinese children.

This exhibit was a three-panel piece; the center panel was larger than the two side panels. It was set up for the side panels to fold over the center panel, covering the entire area if it were closed. All the pictures were in color with captions. I included children's pictures, the cities that we visited, women at work in factories, and some of China's historic sites such as the Forbidden City, the Temple of Heaven, the Palace of Earthly Tranquility, and others.

Although it took me a long time and required hard work to put it together, the exhibit became a piece of art. It was on display for two days in the GSA personnel office, the federal agency that I worked for. Employees thought it was interesting, and they enjoyed looking at it. At Empire State College, where I was attending, the faculty considered it a superior and interesting piece of work. And at their request, it was left on display on the school walls for five years. Thereafter, I donated it to PS-39, a landmark elementary school that my children attended. I recently visited the school, trying to find out if any students had benefited from it. However, since such a long time had gone by, only one member of the school staff, who had been there for thirty years, knew about it. She told me that she knew one student had used it for an assignment, and obviously, I felt happy about that.

All of the above being said, I do realize that my trip to China took place over three decades ago. Since then, there have been significant changes in the country, especially social changes. Nonetheless, the People's Republic of China still is one of the most interesting and visit-worthy countries in the world. I truly enjoyed my trip, and it will forever be the most exciting and educational experience of my life.

Issues at Work

Being active or popular might not always work on your behalf. I will explain why I believe so. I am not trying to tell readers not to be active or not to be popular because these things could benefit them in many ways. Being popular might indicate, among other things, that your contacts with others have left them with a good impression of you. Therefore, people will remember and recognize you at any event or place where you might be. I am not speaking about a celebrity's popularity, but just about an everyday person's popularity. By being active, you demonstrate your ability and desire to get involved in projects and activities to help others or to make a difference in someone's life. Also, by being active you might become popular as well. Having said that, I will suggest that an impression might seem positive to one person, but could be considered negative by another. This is one of the issues I experienced at work. The message that I want to convey is how I managed the situations and how I benefited by them.

Working for thirty years at the same job is an achievement in itself. I do not believe an employer would hold an employee for such a long time unless he or she were a productive and reliable worker, perhaps with some exceptions. An employee should not expect to remain in one place for so long without facing some unwanted or stressful situations. Regardless of who you are or what you do, chances are there could be someone who disagrees with you. During my thirty years in public service, I experienced a number of issues, perhaps too many for me to cite. Though

I did not believe any of the issues were serious, someone else might have had a problem with them. Human nature is difficult to understand, and obviously, I will not even try to explain it. Some employees have problems at home and bring them to their jobs; others have problems at work and bring them home to their families. Actions like these not only affect the person involved, but those around him or her as well.

As I mentioned earlier, I had been working for GSA (a federal agency) since 1966, and in 1976, the agency went through a reorganization that significantly affected many of its employees. As a result, most of them were very upset for they had been downgraded or transferred to other government facilities. While some employees were upset and displaying their anger while at work, I chose to leave before the changes took place. I went to work as a typist for another division within the same agency. Unknown to me, for various reasons I was not being welcomed to my new job by some of the employees. Some of the issues I faced on my new job were somehow justified, and I will explain why.

At the beginning of this chapter, I said that being popular and active does not always work on your behalf. It happened to me, and it could happen to anyone. I have reasons to believe that sometimes popularity could be used against you. And perhaps you don't even know it is happening to you. For example, I was popular at work and at other places where my other duties took place. The furthest thing from my mind was not being welcomed because of my popularity. But it was true. The reason was simple: I was involved in too many activities and events that prevented me from doing my job. Therefore, other employees had to do my work. As for the supervisors, it was a problem having to find somebody to do my work when he or she didn't even want to do his or her own. So they were better off not hiring me. It took me a while to realize what was going on, but when I did, it made sense to me. And while I was not being welcomed by some, I was being called by others because I was popular and good at whatever

I was doing. Of course, I was not going to complain because I liked what I was doing. And there you have the plus and minus of popularity as applied in my case.

Previously I said that common sense and human nature could be used as tools or ways to prevent a small issue from becoming a stressful situation. I believe some of my issues at work were justified, or at least had some merit. Common sense tells you that to be a typist, you should know how to type. I worked as a typist for five years without learning the keyboard, just using two fingers. And on that basis, those who complained about me were correct. Others thought I was courageous for doing what I was doing with my limited knowledge about it. I never felt out of place or uncomfortable about my typing because I had other plans for my future. Some of my coworkers felt that I did not belong there, but it did not bother me. I recognized that, in a way, they were right. As I have said before, sometimes the truth hurts; it might not be hurtful to me, but to someone else, it could easily be.

As time went by, I continued to concentrate on my work, and to my surprise, I was doing very well. Olga, my supervisor, was satisfied with my performance; what mattered to her was my accuracy, not my speed. Olga often told me that my work was better than that of other typists she'd supervised. We developed a friendly relationship, and we often talked about our futures on the job. Olga was not happy with the work habits of some of the employees, and she was hoping to find another job. Once she got to know me, she realized I was going in the right direction for a bright future. She told me the reason that some coworkers seemed not to care for me was because of my popularity and the activities that I was involved with. This is another example of how being popular and active could, in some ways, be used against you. As Olga said to me, "They are jealous of you because they cannot do what you do." And she might have been right.

After five years of typing with two fingers (I still do), I was moved to another position nearby. Though it was not a promotion, I felt good because I did not have to type; I was to write letters to our military service personnel overseas and prepare the necessary documents answering their requests for supplies. This was something that I enjoyed doing, and I did it well. However, now I was closer to my "friends" and had a new supervisor; her name was Anne. Unlike Olga, she was not very friendly.

There was a lady I worked with who liked to watch me; her name was Gladys. She stayed away from everything and everyone because she was not interested in other people's business. Gladys and I became good friends, and we have kept our friendship for the last forty years. Though she is ten years older than I am and we both have grown considerably older than when we worked together, we still have a good time whenever we meet or talk on the telephone. Gladys is a sweet and smart minority woman with a great sense of humor. According to her, I am her only friend because her other ones are either gone or are in nursing homes, waiting for that last day to arrive. She is a good role model for the younger generation.

Gladys says the reason why I became her friend for life is because we had a lot in common; we were both minority women who loved life and enjoyed helping others, and we both had parents who had taught us well. And like me, Gladys struggled and endured difficult experiences in her pursuit of a better life. She was well aware that being a black woman, she most likely would have to work much harder than a man or a nonminority woman to achieve her goals. However, Gladys never let anything get in her way; she knew what she wanted and she worked hard for it. According to her, this was a lesson learned during her childhood.

I believe readers can benefit from Gladys's story by understanding, once again, that success does not come easily, but if they believe in themselves and are ready for the challenge, they too can reach their goals, as Gladys did. Coincidentally, in her younger years, Gladys also owned a brownstone house in a fine neighborhood, as I did. Today, Gladys proudly says that although she's a minority woman, she never had any problems with anyone. She truly believes that the color of your skin is not what matters to most people; it is who you are and how you choose to present yourself to others. She's enjoyed a good life traveling to foreign countries and helping others to improve their quality of life by doing volunteer work in a senior citizens' center.

I am aware that I've digressed from my topic, Issues at Work, but I felt that Gladys's story, which in some aspects is similar to mine, is worthy of reading about, and perhaps, that it could inspire other minority women to find a way to reach their goals. There are some women who would like to improve their quality of life but are afraid to begin their journey due to their fear of failure. Gladys was my coworker and often advised me to continue my search for a better tomorrow.

As time went by and I got to know my coworkers better, based on my own observations and comments made by my supervisor, I was able to understand why they disliked me. It had to do with my popularity and with the many activities that so often kept me away from my work. I never thought it was for being a minority woman, because the majority of the workers were minorities themselves. The fact that I was allowed to get away from my desk and stay away for some time led them to believe that I was getting away with something that they could not. This also gave them a reason to feel jealous of me.

I never paid any attention to what was going on because I was aware of their lack of knowledge about how our system worked. I knew better because I had been trained and instructed on those government rules that allowed me to do what they were complaining about. My absence from work caused more work for them, as well as creating reasons for their complaints. Anne, my supervisor, knew the rules, but at times, she told me that she did not like the idea of me being away from my work so often and for so long. She added that some of my coworkers were complaining. Anne also said to me that it was hard for her to evaluate me when I was away from my work so often. Nonetheless, she had to give me a good evaluation because my performance was highly satisfactory. However, regardless of my performance, she never gave me an "outstanding" evaluation. Obviously, Anne knew that was something she did not have to do, so she did not do it.

One of the activities that I enjoyed the most was being an equal employment opportunity counselor (EEOC). To the best of my recollection, I served as an EEOC for about ten years. And though this might sound like a full-time job, it was not. I never blamed Anne for complaining about the time I was away from my desk. My being allowed to spend as much time as necessary to counsel a complaining employee did not make it easier for her. I do not recall how many counselors my agency had, but there were a few of us. I dare to say that I performed so well as a counselor that some of those complaining employees waited for me to help them. This did not make Anne very happy, and I could understand. But like it or not, it was the system to be blamed, not the employee.

While all of the above was going on, I was getting closer to obtaining my college degree. It was a few years after I'd started working with Anne when I received the call from Professor Kelber letting me know that I had completed all my requirements for my bachelor's degree. In the years before getting my degree, I had applied for other positions within the agency, including that of equal employment opportunity officer. This was a position that I knew I was qualified for. I had been a counselor for many years and had knowledge in other areas within the scope of the position. For example, through my college studies and my active participation in labor unions, I had acquired ample knowledge in the fields of labor and management. Aware that the position could require some higher education, I got a letter from the dean of the

Labor College, which I had been attending, and took it with me to my interview. However, although the dean's letter indicated that I was working on the last nine credits to complete the requirements for my degree, I was not selected for the position. The interviewer told me that the letter did not matter because I still did not have my degree.

I have to admit that this time I was disappointed, so I met with Bill (now deceased), the union shop steward. Some of the things Bill told me during our meeting were hard for me to believe. He said that he had an idea as to why the personnel office would not hire me, and that in his opinion, since they could not admit it, they were using the college degree as an excuse. In his own words, Bill indicated to me that the main reason was my active participation in union activities, as well as in other organizations perceived as not "management-friendly." At the time, I was vice-chairperson for the Hispanic Employment Committee. Bill said that I had two choices: to file a discrimination complaint, or to stay where I was until another position of my choice was announced. By then, I would have my degree. I told him I needed time to think about it and that I would get back to him.

Thereafter, I met with Bill again, and I told him that I would not file a complaint. I explained to him that after thinking about it, I was not sure that had been the reason I hadn't been selected, and so I did not feel comfortable filing a claim. As for my participation in management nonfriendly activities, it could have been, but again, I could not be sure. Besides, if I had been selected as a result of a complaint, I would have created a negative environment starting a new job, and that could not be beneficial to me. So I decided to wait for the next announcement and to be prepared for it. Bill said he respected my decision and that he would offer me his help if needed. Based on this experience, I can tell readers that this is another example of how being popular and active might not work in your behalf.

I continued working with Anne for a few more years before another position I was interested in was announced. This time, it was a building management specialist position. Now I not only had a college degree in labor and management, I also had more experience in dealing with people and in other areas required for the position. Needless to say, I applied for the job and met with Bill. We compared the requirements for the position with my qualifications, including my academic background and my extensive experience in all the required areas. According to Bill, who had ample knowledge on similar issues, there was no one else meeting my qualifications for the position, especially that of my degree. The fact that this position called for career employees from within the agency and within the area was beneficial to me. Bill said that he saw no reason for me not to be selected this time.

I was contacted by the personnel office to let me know that I had been selected for the building management specialist position. I do not remember the exact date when I was informed I had been chosen. But it was just days later when the chief of the unit where I had been working for several years gave me a note. The note indicated the name of the person that I would be reporting to and the date for me to report to the new position. The issue did not end there, however. I was to report the next Monday, so as it is customarily done, on the last Friday before I started the new job, we had a small farewell gathering. And on that same Friday afternoon, while I was clearing my desk, the chief of the unit came to me with another note. This time the note said: "Miss Gomez will not be reporting to PBS on Monday." PBS is Public Building Services, the name of the division. I asked the chief what had happened, and he responded by saying, "They did not tell me the reason." And he walked away.

I immediately called Bill, and since it was time to go home, he told me to see him on Monday morning. He noticed my frustration and said that this time it had nothing to do with me, but with the agency, and that he would explain it to me on Monday. Though I was feeling frustrated and confused, there was nothing I could do but to speak to Bill on Monday. By this time, I really did not know what to believe or what I could possibly do. So I started to prepare myself to perhaps face another difficult situation. There was one thing that I had to keep in mind regardless of the situation—I would be dealing with the government. I had been employed by the federal government for over twenty years, and unfortunately, I had observed some unjust decisions made by the selecting officers. So I wondered if at this time, an unjust decision would be made against me. If a bad decision had been made in my case, the officer in charge could just blame the government and that would be the end of it. That being said, all I could do was to wait and hope for the best, perhaps for a miracle.

On Monday morning, I met with Bill. He was not too happy with what was going on in the personnel office, especially the fact that he would not be able to do anything for me. It was evident that he did not believe them. Their explanation for their action was that the position had been frozen until further notice. I do not recall if they had told Bill whether the action had been taken at the request of the GSA main office in Washington DC, as it is normally done. In other words, the position had not been canceled, but it would remain vacant until the main office decided otherwise. The way in which this action came about gave us reasons to believe something was not right. Bill had ample knowledge about the rules and regulations applied in these cases, and he did not believe their explanation for the action they had taken.

Based on what had happened, there were reasons to believe that something else was going on and that Bill's theory might be right. According to Bill, the personnel officers were certain I would not have been able to challenge such a decision because it was beyond their control. Furthermore, they knew that now I had the college degree, which I did not have in the previous interview. They also were aware that I was highly qualified and that I had expected to be selected. But by using the "position frozen" excuse, they would not have to worry about me challenging their action. Bill always believed it was a discrimination issue, but I did not agree with him. It seemed to me that the selecting officials thought that it could be difficult for me as a manager to deal with labor and management issues because of what my personnel folder revealed about my longtime union activities and my participation in committees such as the Hispanic Employment Committee.

Everything remained unchanged for approximately two more years. Regardless of my disappointment, I continued to do my work and to participate in union activities on behalf of the workers, especially in minority employees' matters. My participation in several organizations in addition to the union and my regular work kept me so involved that I quickly got over my disappointment. I really enjoyed what I was doing, and I was constantly learning something new. Previously, I mentioned that I had been an EEOC for quite some time. Being a counselor offered me great opportunities to learn new things, and most importantly, to meet and help people to solve their complaints concerning discrimination. It made me feel good because it was evident that I was making a difference in some people's lives.

There are several stories that can illustrate what I just said, but I will let the readers enjoy what is, in my opinion, the best of those stories. It was obvious that most, if not all, of those employees who had come to me for help had appreciated whatever I had done for them and they had been telling other employees to see me when they needed some advice. There was one lady whose name was Vera. This woman had been in public service for decades, and according to what other employees and supervisors had told me, she had been complaining and unhappy for just as long. Her personnel folder was so thick that it made you wonder what could have been going on with this woman for so long. During all her years of employment, Vera had worked in different departments within GSA and to the best of my knowledge, in other federal agencies as well. Furthermore, regardless of where or with whom she had worked before, it made no difference to her. She believed nobody liked her and that everybody was trying to get her in trouble.

One day, to my surprise, she came to talk to me. I was surprised because since she hardly spoke to me, I thought that I was the furthest thing from her mind. Vera told me that she needed my help. I had no doubt about what she was looking for, but for the sake of following procedure, I had to ask her what kind of help she needed from me. By now everyone in sight knew what she was looking for; she was using her skin color and her gender to stay away from her duties. She knew she was not going anywhere, but since she had been doing it for so long and no one cared, she kept on doing it.

I do not remember what her response was when I asked her what kind of help she needed from me. But I made an appointment to meet with her at a certain time and date. In the meantime, my coworkers were carefully watching us talking. Everyone thought it was a joke, and they were asking each other what I could possibly do for Vera. Anne, my supervisor, could not believe Vera would ever ask for my help. According to her, Vera had met with people in high-level positions and she had never been satisfied; thus, I would be wasting my time.

Vera and I met, and before she started telling me her reasons for asking me for help, I asked her to listen to what I had to say. I made sure she understood what I could or could not do for her. Most importantly, I explained that I would be very clear and honest with her and that I expected her to understand what I was about to tell her. If at any point of our conversation she did not understand what I was saying, I wanted her to let me know about it and I would explain it to her again. Surprisingly, she agreed with me and then went on to tell me about her complaint. As expected, her main issue was that because she was a woman and she was black, nobody liked her, and therefore she was not being promoted. I told Vera to explain the reasons for her complaint, not her excuses; I wanted to hear facts, not what he or she had said. Her issues were endless, but according to information in her personnel folder, the facts supporting them were not too many.

I am not trying to make readers believe that I read her entire employee folder, for it was not necessary. Though it was thicker than any other one I had seen, a significant part of its information was repeated. It was a long meeting, and we covered a lot of issues that were troubling her. Ironically, Vera felt relaxed and confident that I had been fair to her. I had mentioned to her some of my own experiences and the sacrifices I had endured on my way to a better life. Some of my experiences were similar to hers. Besides being Hispanic, I was a woman. And according to the society in which we both had grown up, women's rights were limited. Therefore, in order for us to search for a better life, we had to work twice as hard compared to nonminority women.

In my opinion, Vera was a smart woman who had endured difficult situations and failures for lack of proper guidance and concerted effort on her part. Sadly, there are some women, not only minority women, who still today endure hardship rather than taking action to improve their quality of life. This might be due to their fear of failure and of not being heard. In Vera's case, after looking at her employee folder, I concluded that the managers in charge were to blame, in part, for allowing her actions to continue for such a long time. I truly believe that it is the government's responsibility to take the necessary action to solve cases like this in a timely manner, before they become a real issue as this one did.

Before ending the meeting, I advised Vera to think about what I had told her and to make a decision for her own good. I also told her not to misunderstand me: I was going to tell her the truth. And I did. The truth was that she could continue with her complaints, but nobody would listen to her anymore. In other words, she was through due to her own actions, but no one would ever tell her so, for fear of possible consequences. I do not remember what transpired after my meeting with Vera because she never contacted me again. Sometime later, I learned that she had been taking time off and had retired. I believe we lost contact with each other because soon after our meeting, I was promoted and moved to another floor far below hers. I never knew if my advice had helped her to make her decision to retire, but I would not have been surprised if it did.

Before going on to another topic, I would like to remind readers that it is up to them to find a way to improve their quality of life. I hope that by reading these stories, readers will be inspired to convince themselves that they can achieve their goals if they want to by listening to good advice and working hard without the fear of failure.

Becoming a Building Manager Specialist

I was promoted to a building manager specialist position two years later. Evidently this was the same position that had been frozen after I had been selected for it and informed about whom to report to and when to start. Unfortunately, a short time before my promotion, something happened unexpectedly that saddened me greatly. Bill, the union shop steward, did not survive a heart attack, and so he never knew about my promotion. All I could do then was to remember some of the things he had said to me two years earlier. He always believed that the reason why I had not been promoted during previous years was because of my effectiveness as a union officer and my involvement in other activities as well. Bill would have been happy to be present to congratulate me for my great achievement.

I cannot say that I agreed or disagreed with Bill's theory about why I had not been promoted. However, after being a manager for a few years, I had reasons to believe that he might have been right. And I dare to say that perhaps, if I had been in the selecting officers' position, I would have done what they did, and I will explain why. When you are a manager or a supervisor, you are in charge of a group of employees. And not only you are in charge, but you are also responsible for what they do and how they do it. Having an employee away from his or her work assignments so often and for so long, as in my case, could create additional burdens for a manager or a supervisor, for the work has to be done with or without the employee assigned to do it.

The manager must be aware that the employee is not at fault as long as the system allows the situation to go on. When I say *employee*, in this case it is me, and the *system* is federal employment. The way in which the federal sector practices the duties that kept me away from my assigned duties could not be practiced in the private sector. The duties exist in private employment, but as regular paid positions. In my case, there were too many duties keeping me away from my job. I can honestly say that at times, I had sympathized with my supervisor, but I was simply following the rules. Based on my experiences and observations, some of the activities in which I was involved should be considered full-time jobs. But that is not the way it is in the federal sector.

There were instances when I was away from my work for the entire day. And since my regular work had to be done, other employees had to do it for me, though some of them could hardly keep up with their own assignments. The situation obviously created a problem for my supervisor. That being said, it explains the reasons why some employees did not welcome me to work with them, and the reason why I had not been promoted to higher positions for a long time. However, the situation was of my own choice. Since I liked what I was doing and I was doing it so well and the system allowed me to do it, I kept on doing it.

Becoming a building manager specialist was one of my best achievements. I never imagined it was going to be easy, but I was ready for the challenge. There was no doubt that I needed to make a complete turnaround and that I had a lot to learn. Furthermore, I would not be able to participate in union activities anymore. Resigning my union membership was not easy for me, but I had no choice. In fact, the personnel office made it simple for me to resign: they cancelled my membership immediately and without saying a word to me. As a manager, I had to resign my previous duties so I could concentrate on my new job. I knew I had a lot to learn, but I had no problem. Almost the entire building population knew who I was, and they were all wishing me well and were happy to work with me in work-related issues of their concern.

I remember the top judge in the Court of International Trade, who was very hard to please. No manager liked to take his call because he was just too difficult. So one day my boss, Frank, told me he was going to send me to the judge. Frank had a good sense of humor. The judge had called for something, but I don't remember what it was. Frank said, "Go see what he wants and let me know." I went to his office, and I believe I said, "Hello, sir, what can I do for you?" I told him who I was, and very politely he said, "I welcome you, and now I should have no problem getting things done." When I told Frank the judge had fallen in love with me, he could not believe that judge having love for anybody. Since that day, I owned a judge.

Some of my coworkers were in the wait-and-see mode, thinking it would be something difficult for me to do. As for me, what they were thinking was the least of my concerns. In fact, I had no concerns. At home everything was fine. Freddy was very busy, like me, going through his own issues at work. After earning his college degree, he was being promoted to higher positions with greater responsibilities. As for issues at work, everything was fine as well. Freddy also never worried about my issues at work because he knew the way the system worked and that I knew how to handle it.

Peter Jr. was married and gone, Emmaline was doing very well in college, and Benedicta was minding her own business at the hospital as a nurse. The big family of yesterday had gone away, leaving behind an almost empty big house.

I had been around for a long time, and I was familiar with most of the tenant agencies within the building. Besides being much older than most of the others, including my boss, Frank, I had experienced good and not-so-good situations before. I knew that I would not have any problem dealing with the people from other agencies or with the general public. Dealing with people was one thing I had been doing through my participation in the different activities and events.

I was confident that I could do the job as a manager, but I would not feel relaxed until learning what my assignment would be. However, it did not matter because for the first few years, I would be a trainee. All building manager trainees must learn some of the basic aspects related to the overall maintenance of buildings. Also, a manager must be able to deal with the general public, government officials, and other projects and activities too numerous for me to cite. Obviously, I am talking about federal building managers, not managers of private buildings.

I went through the training without major difficulties. Every three months, I met with the training officer for a general evaluation. He asked me about the items I'd covered during the previous three months, and then he analyzed my answers. I also had an opportunity to ask questions and to let him know of any concerns that I might have. My response to one of the officer's questions during the first three- month meeting was one that I could never forget. He said, "Let's make believe you were in charge of the cleaning maintenance of a building and there was a specific area within the building that needed cleaning urgently. You were to assign an employee to the task and give him or her specific instructions about how you needed the work to be done, as well as the expected time of completion. However, the employee did not follow your instructions, his performance was unsatisfactory, and the time was running out." The officer wanted to know what action I would take in such a situation in order to complete the task satisfactorily and on time. I responded by saying that I would do it myself. This was not the correct answer, but it was the first thing that came to my mind.

The officer did not like my response and went ahead explaining to me what a manager's responsibility really was and how an efficient manager gets things done. He said that at no time should the manager do the work of a subordinate; he or she was there to get the work done through the subordinates, not by doing it herself or himself.

Although the first three-month meeting was not easy for me, I can say that it was very productive. I believe it was at this event that I learned what being a manager really meant. Thereafter, I felt good and relaxed when meeting with the training officer. As time went by, I was increasing my knowledge of things that I had never done before. I liked my job, and according to comments and letters from tenants, I was doing a commendable job.

I can proudly say that I developed a friendly and professional relationship with my supervisors. They knew I was a dependable and responsible employee who always tried to do her best. Regardless of the nature of the assignment, they could count on me to obtain good results. Frank, my supervisor at the time, used to say that I should not have a problem managing a government building because I had been effectively managing a hundred-year-old brownstone house. Frank did not hesitate to put me in charge of the cleaning crew and other less important areas when the time came to assign me my specific areas of responsibility.

The cleaning crew had its unique problems, and there were a large number of employees. In addition to GSA (government) workers, the cleaning staff also had contract employees. Needless to say, I was the right manager for the job. I do not mean to say it was such a difficult task, but it called for someone with natural virtues such as tons of patience, an easygoing nature, and a friendly personality. I was blessed with all of them. I consider myself a people's person. And though dealing with people is not an easy task, I do it just by being myself.

Most of the things mentioned above do not require any specific level of education. We do not need to go to college to learn to be patient, easygoing, or friendly. These are personal characteristics that make you a better person, and some people have them and don't even know that they do. So chances are that some readers could have some, if not all, of these virtues. That being said, I would like to advise readers to help themselves to find a way to discover whatever natural virtues they might possess and to use them to improve their quality of life. It might not be so simple to do, but it might work.

I can continue telling readers about my good and not-so-good stories and the events that I experienced as a manager. But for the sake of not overdoing it, I will tell them just those that I consider the best and that can convey a message to them.

I was doing very well in my training, without major difficulties. And since trainees are required to visit other government facilities as part of their training, I was sent to visit a facility in Bayonne, New Jersey. I tried to have someone do the driving for me, to no avail. I was really afraid to drive by myself, but there was no choice. David, my supervisor at the time, told me it was no big deal: just keep to my right when possible and watch my speed on the turnpike. I must have had someone from above watching me because I made it back safely. However, I experienced something that, although common on the roads, had never happened to me before. As soon as I returned to the office, I told David that at one point while on the turnpike, I had been in the wrong lane to make my turn. As I reduced my speed and tried to get into the right lane, another driver got very upset and called me an "SOB" driving a "damned" government car. David just said, "That happens all the time."

The next time I had to go to New Jersey, I got Ralph from the maintenance crew to do the driving for me. The traffic was heavy and it was getting late, and Ralph, concerned about the time, crossed the yellow double line in the Holland Tunnel. We were lucky that nothing happened and we got away without a ticket, but I was nervous and I told Ralph not to do it ever again. Ralph said he was sorry and that he was just trying to get me to the facility on time. He added that since it was a government car, nobody would bother us. I told Ralph that he was living on a different planet. And last but not least, one day I was driving on the Brooklyn-Queens Expressway and the traffic was very heavy. It was a stop-and-go situation. All of a sudden, I felt something fall on my lap and my heart skipped a beat. The car's steering wheel had fallen off. I quickly put it back on, but you cannot imagine how scared I was. When I told David he said, "Sometimes it happens."

Thereafter, I did not have to drive anymore. I had completed my training and was working full time on my assignments. One morning as I walked into the office, Frank asked me to come to see him. He wanted to tell me that Mr. Gooding, the cleaning crew supervisor, had complained to him about something I had said during my meeting with him the previous day. Frank never thought that I had purposely said something offensive to Mr. Gooding because he knew me better than that. Regardless, it was his responsibility to talk to me about it. I thought hard about it, but I could not remember saying anything offensive. Then Frank asked me, "While talking to Mr. Gooding about the maintenance workers, did you refer to them as "your people?" I said, "Yes. And what was wrong with that?" Then Frank told me, "Be cautious with the words you use when speaking to minorities. There are some terms that are considered offensive." And I thanked Frank for teaching me a great lesson.

The next morning, I called Mr. Gooding to come to my office. We discussed our misunderstanding of the day before and how to prevent future ones. Also, I made him aware of the fact that I was there to work with him, not to work against him. It was decided that future disagreements could be resolved between the two of us, without having to go to Frank. As time went by and the employees got to know me better, we developed a good working relationship, which lasted until my retirement. I enjoyed working with them, and they all trusted and respected me. So, the "your people" event was quickly forgotten. But Frank's simple lesson, I never forgot.

Frank called me to his office one more time, but it had nothing to do with the workers. There were occasions when people in the film industry requested permits for filming in federal buildings. These events were not welcomed by any of the building managers, and they explained why to me. They told me that when the filmmakers requested the permits, they couldn't tell us how many hours they needed; they could only estimate. And according to the managers, in the past, these people had remained in the building into the night hours. Therefore, before I issued the permit, I was to make sure a manager would be there until they finished for the day. Since no manager was willing to do it, I would have to stay until they were finished for the day.

One day, a member of Oliver Stone's staff came to the building manager's office to get a permit to do some filming for the movie *Wall Street* in the lobby of the building. I signed the permit and agreed to remain in the building for as long as necessary. Since federal buildings are public buildings, we are not allowed to charge for their use as long as a building manager signs a permit. As companies receive the permit, most of them insist on making a payment or on giving something to the manager in charge in appreciation. We could not accept gifts, but monetary donations for the building are accepted. The day of the event came and the filming took place, ending at 8:00 p.m.

The next morning, as I walked into the building, Frank called me to his office. Someone had told him that I had accepted some money from the film crew. According to the person who had talked to Frank, I had received two white envelopes with money and had turned over just one to security. He needed to know what had happened because if I had accepted money, I could have been in big trouble. Obviously I was disturbed, but I did not lose control. I was able to give Frank a clear and credible response to his question.

I never thought that Frank believed what he had been told about me. We had known each other for a long time, and he had complete trust and confidence in me. I never got to know who the accuser was, but it did not matter to me. I was aware that things like that happened, and the accuser's mistrust of me did not mean anything to me. Sometimes unhappy or frustrated people test the new manager's strength for any future event involving the manager. Thereafter, everything was taken care of, although I do not remember the details. The accusation was untrue and never put in my file. What I accepted from the film crew was a Chinese dinner at the building's plaza, which was okay because of the late hours.

I served as a manager for ten years, and during that time I experienced incidents and events of different kinds; coincidentally, Freddy was going through similar experiences on his new job as a manager.

As previously mentioned, I was responsible for the cleaning crews, government workers, and contract workers. Though not too many managers enjoyed overseeing these employees, I dare to say that somehow, I enjoyed it. One of the reasons why I felt that way was because I knew they did not fear me when I went to check their performance. At the beginning, they did not feel too comfortable with my visits, but once they got to know me, they relaxed. When I spoke to them, they liked it because they knew I was trying to help them in any way I could. Ironically, they did not mind even when I had to tell them that their performance was poor. I understood why some managers did not feel the way I did; they had nothing in common with these employees, which made it difficult for both parties to develop a good working relationship. The workers' impression of me was that I could have been one of them, that I could "speak their language." I can share with my readers how a situation that's difficult for one person could be simple for someone else.

The contract workers were under a special program: "The Federation of the Handicapped." Under this program, in order to be hired, every one of them had to suffer from some kind of handicap, and there were many employees. The government workers did not have to be handicapped, but many of them were "socially" handicapped. All of the above being said, some readers might sympathize with the managers for feeling the way they did. Situation like these could really seem like a nightmare for anyone. You might not need a college degree to perform well, but patience and common sense you could not do without. As I said earlier, I was blessed by having lots of patience and a friendly personality, and I was easygoing. The following incidents, in my opinion, are of a kind that perhaps could make readers wonder how I was able to get away with what I did.

Leon was one of the government maintenance workers who was addicted to liquor, and I am sure you know what I mean. When it was official that I would be in charge of the maintenance crew, other managers and supervisors warned me about possibly having trouble with him, and they advised me the best they could. He was a fairly young and strong-looking black fellow, who most of the time, used to hide in the bathrooms while on duty. His performance was poor, and so was his work record. In other words, there was no hope for Leon. It seemed as if everyone had given up on him; however, some of his coworkers used to help him with his assignments because, after all, he was not a bad person.

Regardless of all the negative information I had been given about Leon, I was hoping to meet him soon, and without any concerns. Meanwhile, he had been told about me by his coworkers and supervisors, just as I had been told about him by my own staff. But he was not concerned because he did not recognize my name. As there was no reason for me to be around his areas of work before I became a manager, I did not know who he was. When we met he appeared in control, and he studied me as if he were trying to find out if I had been told about his problems.

His physical appearance was disgusting. He had an Afro haircut, which made his head look three times its normal size. His white uniform shirt was dirty and food stained. Obviously, he knew what he had been doing was wrong and he felt embarrassed. By what he said to me during our meeting and by the way he looked at me, I got the impression that he was a smart man who needed a lot of help. I was confident that I could bring out the best in him. My story about Leon is long, but the most important part is the ending, and I will explain it.

Soon after I gained his confidence and I knew him better, I felt it was time for a straight talk with him. Readers may wonder about how I got away with saying the very personal things that I said to him without getting him upset. One of the things I would like readers to keep in mind in reading my book is that in most cases, it is not what you say but how you say it; believe me, this theory works. When we met, the first thing I did was to ask Leon if he were ready and willing to hear the truth from me; I warned him that he might find some of the things I was going to say offensive and embarrassing. I said that if he were not ready, we should not waste our time, because in my opinion, I saw no other way out for him than to make a complete turnaround. He said he was ready to hear what I had to say.

Leon was eager to hear me talk. I asked him, "Leon, do you like what you see when you look at yourself in a mirror?" He responded by saying, "I do not look good." Then I asked him, "Do you want to look good?" He just said, "Yes." I continued asking him other questions, and he appeared relaxed. Toward the end of our meeting, I mentioned to him some of the most important things he must do to look like the real Leon. He was to get a haircut, wear a clean white shirt, shave his beard, and stop his drinking. The last thing I said to him was that it would make me happy if when I looked at him, I saw a handsome young man rather than a monster. He promised me he was going to do his best to look good to make me proud of him. As for his drinking, he needed more time, but he was going to start working on it.

I do not remember how soon after that meeting I saw him again. One day, he called my office and asked if he could come to see me, that he had a big surprise for me. When he entered the office, he looked great. My coworkers could not believe their eyes; he had gone through a complete turnaround. He had cut his hair and shaved his beard, and his white shirt was white. He walked over to my desk saying, "Surprise," and then he asked me, "Could I give you a hug, Mom?" He liked to call me Mom; he used to say it made him feel good. I don't recall what I said to him at the moment, for he looked so different and so happy. After the hug, he also asked me if he could call me his "white mother." From then on, there was no turning back for him. He was seriously working on getting rid of his drinking habit, at least while on duty.

As time went by, Leon kept his promise to stay clean and to improve his performance and physical appearance 100 percent. When I started to plan my retirement, he was not too happy, and he asked me if he could call me at home when he had a problem. After I left, he called me at home several times and also came to visit me. He wanted me to know how much he appreciated all I had done for him and that he would remember me forever. I can honestly say that I consider Leon's story one of my great achievements—helping a lost human being to come back to enjoy life with dignity and resolve.

Leon was certainly a success story, and indeed one of my best achievements. He kept his promise and was promoted to better positions in building maintenance. The last time we spoke, he told me he was considering applying for a building manager position. He wanted to hear what I had to say. I told him that alone was good news, but first he had to show what he had to offer. And under the circumstances, it was only wishful thinking. He understood.

Feliciano was another government worker with big problems. He was out constantly, and when he came in to work, he was late. He used to report to work so intoxicated that he could hardly walk, and he also fell asleep in the bathrooms. He had been written up and counseled repeatedly, but nothing had worked. One day he came in to work so impaired that his supervisor sent him to me to take the proper action. Once I saw him, I knew he had to go because we had already complied with the rules applied to this kind of behavior from an employee. I explained to him the procedures that management had followed, and that as a result, he had to go. To my surprise, he responded by saying that he understood and that I was doing the right thing. After he returned from the personnel office, he came back to me, shook my hand, and thanked me for letting him go.

Incidents like this rarely happen, but at times they do. We often hear people ask, "How could this happen?" If we compare the way the Leon and Feliciano incidents were resolved, using a different approach to a similar situation, we could also ask, "Why?" There is no specific answer to these questions. All I can tell readers is that, as previously mentioned, human nature is difficult to comprehend, and no one can explain it with a high degree of certainty. Leon and Feliciano are good examples of human nature at its best.

The following is one of my most unforgettable and unique experiences as a building manager. Sometimes an employee who does something far and beyond his or her duties is recognized by receiving a "fast-track award," a small amount of money. There was construction going on outside the federal building, and the field mice were being disturbed. Therefore, they were looking for a new home, and they came to our building and entered the child care center located in the lobby of the building. When the children and their teacher saw one of them running around, they were afraid and immediately called the building manager's office. As part of my duties, I responded to the call.

I called the maintenance supervisor and asked him to have one of his employees meet me at the center. As I entered the room, I found the children on top of the tables because they were afraid of mice. They showed me where the mouse was hiding. It was behind a wall cabinet so I held an opened plastic bag at one end of the cabinet while the employee held another opened plastic bag at the other end. The mouse quickly ran into my bag and it was caught. Days later, I got another call from the teacher about another mouse in the center. We caught the second mouse using the same procedure we had used before. For catching the two mice, I was presented a fast-track award," a fifty-dollar check. From then on, I was known as the mice catcher. Some employees could not believe I had caught the two mice; they thought it had been a heroic act. But for me, it was just a simple and effortless event.

My Children

Peter and Emmaline have been my life's greatest achievements. They are worthy of all my sacrifices, worries, and pains—even some of my gray hair. I cannot imagine what my life would have been like without them, especially as I get older. They are thirteen years apart, and some friends and relatives have asked me why there was so much time in between. For personal reasons, I have never given them a straight answer, but there were plenty of reasons. Some of them have been explained in previous chapters of my book. After enduring the difficult and painful situation during and after Peter Jr. was born, I was not ready to make plans of any kind. For me, planning another child was unimaginable at the time. However, I would like to tell my readers that my pain and suffering were only emotional, and almost always, I kept them to myself. Violence was never an issue in the disagreements I had with my husband, and we never argued in public either. Furthermore, when we discussed any particular issue, we both remained in control and never displayed any anger while our little boy was present.

When I learned that another child was coming, I was surprised, and I quickly told Peter, wondering what his reaction would be. His quick reaction was not what I had hoped; instead of inspiring a happy moment, it clearly demonstrated a complicated and insecure future for both of us. Meanwhile, I was already feeling love for that precious human being growing inside me. From then on, we did not talk about my condition unless he mentioned it.

And when he did, some of the things he said did not make me happy. I thought that perhaps he felt all my love and attention would be for the new baby and none for him, just as he had felt when Peter Jr. was born.

I was feeling healthy and happy planning for the event that was rapidly approaching. As I mentioned earlier, Peter Jr. and my friends were excited about the new baby coming and were making their own plans to help me care for it. The baby was born, and when we were told it was a little girl, we quickly fell in love with her, even though we had been expecting a boy. Our lives went on just fine, and everything seemed under control. No one had been thinking about a baby girl, but there she was, as beautiful as a flower.

I came back home with my little daughter, and my neighbors and friends were happy for us. But the happiest ones were Peter Jr. and his friends. Then I realized that my children being thirteen years apart had been a blessing for me. Peter Jr. loved to care for his sister, and he knew how to do it. He was thirteen years old at the time. Though my husband did not show too much emotion with the new baby, he also helped me to care for her.

I am proud of my two children as my parents were proud of their ten. From their early childhood, I taught my children well, as my parents did to me. And although times had changed drastically and they were born in different decades, my children knew that respect and good behavior should not change with time. Most parents say they are proud of their kids and do not hesitate to defend them when they get in trouble. They feel it is their responsibility to help their child, that he or she is a good kid. And almost always they believe their child did not do anything wrong. But where are the facts? Shouldn't they get the facts before condoning the child's acts? I agree it is the parents' responsibility to help their children by teaching them respect and good behavior and to avoid getting in trouble. Saying something to a child while doing something else could confuse the child.

When Peter Jr. was fifteen years old, he had an experience that he will never forget. In the early seventies, the New York City subway system had revolving turnstiles, where you had to insert a token to get on the train. Since the turnstiles were big enough to fit more than one person, teenagers used to go in by the bunch with just one token. This act was called "jumping the turnstiles." The police could arrest those caught in the act and punish them according to their age and their previous violations. Peter Jr. had confessed to me that he was doing it with his friends when the police officers were not around. I told him to stop doing it because if he were caught, I would let him sleep in jail one night. He did not believe I would do that to him because he knew that I loved him so much.

Peter did not take me seriously, and he and a few friends ended up getting caught by the police. Everyone else ran away, but Peter remained with the officer, giving his name and age and my work telephone number. The officer called me, explained to me what had happened, and asked me what I wanted him to do with Peter. I told the officer to put him in jail for one night because I had warned him about it several times and he needed to learn a lesson. The officer said to me he did not have to do that because Peter had promised him he wouldn't do it again. He advised Peter to keep his promise and to stay away from trouble. After talking to me, he believed Peter would never do it again. The officer let Peter go and told me that I should be proud of my son.

Peter Jr. developed into a handsome and charming young man with a friendly personality. He did well in school, and most of his teachers loved him. The only problem with him was that he talked too much. But his grades were high and he never got into any kind of trouble through all his school years. After high school, he entered Brooklyn College and dropped out after the first year. He told me college was not for him and that he was not going back. I told him that he had only two choices: staying in school or getting a job. His response was that he would find a job. He had been working since he was thirteen years old, and he liked to work rather than go to school. When he was thirteen and for several years after that, after school hours, he had worked as a counselor in a church for kids of his age and younger.

Peter Jr. was the perfect role model for young children. He was never in trouble, though he was exposed to many temptations. He was everyone's friend. Parents liked his friendly approach to their children. Basically, his job was to counsel young children to walk away from trouble and to do well in school. In humorous tones he demonstrated to them how Mother disciplined him. He showed how Mother grabbed his ear saying, "I will keep twisting until you listen to me and do what I tell you." Peter Jr. summarized, "Mother meant it and I obeyed. And here I am, happy and clean as a whistle. So listen to Mom and Dad, and you will do well."

At the age of twenty-one, Peter Jr. took four tests with the New York City Transit Authority and did well in all of them. He was put on a waiting list of several thousand applicants, and when he was twenty-four, he was hired as a train conductor for the New York City subway system. After thirty-one years of service, he retired at the age of fifty-five. Now at home with his wife, Sonia, he enjoys life doing what he loves to do, listening to his music, playing with his Chihuahua, and playing his drums—something he has been doing since he was a young boy.

Peter Jr. is proud of me and appreciates the things I do for him. He has promised me he will take care of me when I can no longer take care of myself. He feels that it is the least he can do for me after all I have done for him. In today's society, there is an important thing that seems to have been forgotten; that important thing is called respect. Peter Jr. has never disrespected me, not even once in his life. If he disagrees with me on anything, he tells me about it, but he always respects my opinion. These are some of the many reasons for me to be proud of my son.

In a previous chapter, I told readers about my divorce from Peter's father. Unfortunately, after the divorce there was a poor relationship between father and son. After Peter left New York, he called Peter Jr. several times, almost always to talk about me. But some of the words he used while asking about me upset Peter Jr. He told his father not to call again if he did not have anything nice to say about his mother. Communication between the two of them stopped, and to this date, father and son do not communicate with each other. I recently contacted Peter and invited him to come and visit Peter Jr., but he said he would only do it if he were invited by his son, not by me. His reaction indicates poor judgment, selfishness, and a lack of responsibility on his part.

As for Peter Jr., with my love and support, he has enjoyed a good life. At the present time, he is enjoying his retirement and helping me cope with my daily chores. Some of my neighbors and friends tell me that I am lucky to have a son like Peter. But I know it was not luck; it was the way he was raised. He is not perfect; if he were, he would not be human. Today I am proud of him and also proud of myself for teaching him well, just like my parents taught me.

Emmaline did not have much to say about her father because she was too young to remember him and to understand what went on after her father left us behind when she was only seven. Though not often, they do communicate with each other. With my love and support, Emmaline grew up to be a respected, responsible, and successful career woman. Unlike her brother, Emmaline chose to leave home. She has been successful in every place she has gone. She finally made Texas her home, where she is happily living with her husband, Aaron, and their pride and joy, Gavin. I can honestly say that I am proud of my daughter for reaching her goals amid some degree of uncertainty and sacrifice.

GAVIN

Gavin is my only grandchild; though he is six years old, he still seems to me like a dream and a blessing. I had considered being a grandmother as my only unreachable goal. My daughter was reaching a difficult age to have a first child, and I was already at an advanced age. This made it difficult for me to be with her as much as I would have liked to be. So I had given up my hopes of being a grandmother.

One day, Emmaline and her husband came to visit me, and on the way home from the airport, she told me that she was expecting. I made believe I had not heard what she had said, so her husband repeated it to me. I thought they were kidding. It took me a while to believe it and to put my thoughts together. It was obvious to me that I had to undo my plans and rethink what I had thought about my future. And one more time, I knew my sister Benedicta would be there for me, to help me plan my new life as a grandmother.

From then on, time went so fast for me it seemed as if everything were in a rush to come and go. I was concerned about the possible danger to Emmaline and her baby because of factors related to her age. Every time she called me, my heart skipped a beat, but I kept it to myself.

One evening about seven o'clock, Aaron called to let us know that he had taken Emmaline to the hospital. He tried his best not to frighten me, but I was very concerned for the health of mother and baby. The fact that we were so far apart made the situation more difficult for me. But regardless of the situation, Freddy and I immediately contacted the airlines to purchase tickets to Texas. We arrived in Texas in the early morning hours and went directly to the hospital. And there she was, looking good and happily awaiting her little boy to enter her world. But it did not happen. So she came back home.

Emmaline felt the symptoms of the real thing a few days later, and back to the hospital we went. This time it was for real: Gavin was born. I was by Emmaline's side during and after the arrival of her beautiful baby. Watching my grandchild coming into this world was not easy for me. I felt a deep pain in my heart seeing my daughter going through so much pain, and I prayed silently for her pain to go away. Suddenly everything seemed normal, and I was about to experience some of the most precious moments of my life. When I held the baby in my arms, all pain disappeared. I felt the beginning of a new life—and it certainly has been.

Freddy returned home after two weeks, but I remained with Emmaline for the next two months. Then my daughter returned to work, and Benedicta arrived to care for Gavin. She still cares for him today. Due to my responsibilities at home and my health condition, I have only made short visits every few months, but Gavin not only turned my life around—he gave me a new reason for living. He is a picture of love and happiness, and he is intelligent and handsome. I call him "my angel."

My stories about Gavin are good examples of what I have been saying in my book. His good manners and his good behavior wherever he goes demonstrate the caliber of life he experiences at home. It is a reflection of the childhood lessons learned at home. Evidently his parents are teaching him well, similar to what I did to his mother and what my parents did to me. These are reasons to believe that Gavin will teach his own children well when he gets to be a father. This is the message that I have tried to bring to the attention of parents with young children.

As I have mentioned before, no child is born knowing anything. Gavin was not born knowing good manners and good behavior; he was taught so by his parents during his early childhood. By the time he entered school, Gavin was well prepared and ready to start his schoolwork. As a result, learning has become easier for him, setting him up in the right direction for a productive future. We should all know that building a strong base is the utmost important part of anything we do. In the field of education, the principle is the same. And although Gavin is just in the first grade, his strong base has already been built. He is beginning to understand the importance of a good education. Obviously, this is the reason why at the age of six he is already talking about going to college.

I have been using Gavin as an example because of what I have been saying since I started my writing. I have told readers that all statements and opinions mentioned in my book do not come from statistics, but from my own experiences and observations. I also told the readers about the importance of a well-balanced childhood in a child's development, and the role of parents. I have observed Gavin throughout his young life, and he is a clear example of my message to readers and parents as well. Needless to say, his parents are a perfect example of the parents' responsibility and the role they should play in the development of their children. It will make a big difference in the children's lives as they reach adulthood. It will not only benefit the child; it could also help teachers and other students in the classroom. A student with bad behavior might interrupt the learning process, making it difficult for other students to learn their lessons. It has been said that an apple does not fall too far from the tree, and almost always it's true.

Almost every day, we hear of horrible crimes being committed by young children. But what we do not hear is about the whereabouts of their parents. Although parents are responsible for their children's behavior, they rush to blame somebody else for their children's actions. If we were to compare the home environment of a misbehaving child with that of Gavin, the difference would be night and day. Gavin was, and still is, well taught at home. One important thing that some parents fail to realize is that by observing a child, in most cases, one can have an idea of what his or her home environment is like. A child's behavior could reflect the family's lifestyle, which if based on the child's bad behavior, almost always that lifestyle has been a negative influence on the child. So I hope that in reading this book, parents will give a thought to some of the things I have said over and over in my stories above. By doing so, I trust they will learn something from it and pass it on to their children for the benefit of all.

Friends tell me my daughter is lucky she has her family's support. And that is true. Although my sister Benedicta and I live in New York, and Emmaline lives in Texas, we have been there for her. Our support not only helps my daughter; it is of utmost importance to her child. Benedicta stays with Emmaline most of her time, coming home for short periods of time during the summer and the Christmas holidays. Freddy and I often visit for some periods of time as well. It does not create any hardship for the family, for we are all well-set and retired.

A GOOD LIFE

Life is beautiful. Most people love it and try to make the best of it, while others waste it foolishly. I often wonder what incites a person to take someone else's life. We all know that we have only one life, which cannot be replaced by anything or anyone. It cannot be brought back once someone takes it from you. Though aware of these facts, some people still take other people's lives and think nothing of it. It seems to me that ending someone's life is considered by our society as just an unfortunate part of our everyday lives, but that's absolutely untrue. There is no reason nor a logical explanation for committing such a devastating and unlawful act.

Horrible crimes are committed daily, and we hear about them in the news and from people everywhere we go. But no matter where we go or whom we hear it from, everyone seems to ignore, in my opinion, the most important factor of the crimes being committed. I am certain that not every reader or listener will agree with me, because I firmly believe that the important factor goes back to the parents. We all know that every human being has, or had, a father and a mother. Where are they when their young son or young daughter commits crimes? Chances are they will come out to tell us that their child is innocent and would never do such a thing, because he or she is a good kid. Do they believe their child will enjoy a good life by committing crimes? I don't think so. This brings me back to my childhood and the lessons learned from my parents.

162

My parents taught me to respect others and to stay away from trouble. They made me understand that everything in life has a price. If I wanted something, I had to earn it. We never expected to get anything for nothing. Things that I learned from my parents, I passed on to my children. Today, my daughter is teaching her child those important things she learned during her childhood. Gavin is a perfect example of what the parents can do to help a child get on the right path to be successful and to enjoy a good life in the future. All children come into this world the same way. And regardless of their color or religion, there is no difference in what they do and in what they need. As children begin life in a new environment, their learning process begins. They are ready to learn what they observe and what they hear. So it is at this point that the parents should accept their responsibility to teach their children well. Such an upbringing is the best gift a parent could ever give a child.

Based on my observations of young children, including my own, I would like to remind readers that I do believe that what we learn during childhood stays with us forever. It could also be a factor in our future quality of life. If a child is given the opportunity to develop a strong base during his or her first years, it is easier for the child to achieve his or her goals during adulthood. If parents do not make this happen, children can become vulnerable a long life of confusion and difficulties. It is my opinion, since I am not an expert on child development and behavior, that today's parents are not aware of the fact that children begin their learning endeavor as soon as they enter this world.

In addition, most parents do not consider childhood as the most important stage in child development. As a result, children are left at the mercy of those around them, making it easier for the children to be confused and prone to begin their development in the wrong environment. Such a situation might create a negative pattern that could make it difficult for the child to enjoy a good life as he or she becomes an adult. Again, I hope that parents, especially those with young children, read my book and learn something from it. I have tried to do my best by writing it in simple language, using examples and providing plenty of details for a better understanding of the message that I am trying to convey to the readers.

I can proudly say that I have enjoyed a good and productive life. Regardless of my struggles and sacrifices mentioned in previous chapters, I have managed to maintain a good quality of life. The fact that I have accomplished so much with so little has made some of my friends and relatives wonder how I did it. Good things might not come easy, but you will never know how far you can go unless you start your journey. I started my journey to a better life when I was twenty-five years old. I had been married for four years and had a child. From then on, I never looked back. Though young and inexperienced in serious matters, with the help of my husband, I purchased my first home in New York City. And I trust the readers remember from previous chapters the story about my brownstone house. Peter was not too happy about facing such a great responsibility, but I never doubted that we could do it. I knew that I had to work hard to maintain my home, and I was not afraid of it. My parents had told me that if I wanted something, I had to work for it. So I did, and as a result, I enjoyed my home for forty-five years.

After purchasing the brownstone house, my sister Benedicta and I bought a summer home in the village of Fleischmanns in New York's Catskill Mountains. This was the thrill of my life, especially the mountains. It was a place to relax while enjoying nature at its best. And most of all, the mountains meant so much to me, for they brought back childhood memories. On weekends and holidays, along with friends and relatives, I walked through the mountains, went swimming, and attended auctions and other events too many to cite. My family and I enjoyed nature's beauty in every season. And we lived some of the most precious moments of our lives in the peaceful and relaxing environment of the Catskill Mountains.

Benedicta and I owned the house for twenty years. Then we had to sell our unforgettable home in the mountains due to matters beyond our control. Children grew up and went their own ways. We got older and had to accept the reality of changes in our lifestyle. Nevertheless, the memories of those twenty years of good and happy living will remain with us until the end of time. Today, though not often, we still enjoy visiting the small village of Fleischmanns. In the following chapter, I will let my readers know how I did it all, to the best of my recollection.

How I Did It All

I do not believe that my achievements were a matter of luck or because of help from others. Some people seriously believe that luck can help you get to where you are going and also to get what you want. And I respect their beliefs. However, for me, luck is something intangible that we wish to others and for ourselves to make people feel good. The dictionary offers plentiful meanings for this word, but after all is said, it is only a wish. So I must tell readers that I cannot give luck the credit for my achievements. The credit goes to my commitments and my hard work.

My desire to make a difference in other people's lives began when I was in my early teenage years. At thirteen I was already making, or fixing, my school uniforms and those of friends and neighbors. My knowledge of sewing was so advanced that I was able to make my graduation-day dresses for my junior high school and high school graduations. I also did some sewing for neighbors at the modest charge of twenty-five or thirty-five cents per piece of clothing. However, most of the time I did not receive any payment for my work because they just could not afford it. I understood their situation and I continued to help them, though aware of the fact that they could not afford to pay me.

What I did with the school uniforms was something unique. I cannot recall where the idea came from, but I believe it was Mother's idea. I believe one of my younger sisters also fixed her uniforms the way I did mine, but I do not remember which one of them it was. My parents could only afford to purchase one uniform skirt for each one of us, excluding the three older sisters because they were no longer at home. The uniform skirt was pleated and of burgundy color. We wore the uniform for the entire school year, often washing and ironing it. As a result, it looked worn, more so on the file of the pleats. So I took the skirt apart and put it back together with its inside out. Since both sides of the fabric were identical, I was able to hide the worn parts while making the new pleats. The uniform looked just like new, giving me the feeling of a new uniform for the new school year. What I did saved me from embarrassment from the other students who could afford a new uniform, and also from creating a financial burden for my parents.

Although the school-uniform experience did not seem like a great achievement to me, it was indeed the beginning of something much greater and of utmost importance for my future. The lesson to be learned could have been to live within your limits or to do more with less. These are things that when we are young, most of us do not think about, or perhaps do not understand. Nevertheless, they are put aside in our minds for future use. When I did what I did to my school uniform, I was just thinking about looking like the rest of the students without being embarrassed. I never imagined that behind my action there were lessons to be learned that would also be useful to me as I reached adulthood. Though to live within your limits is an important factor for a stress-free life, most people do not practice it. I am proud to say that it has been, and still is, a common practice within my family.

I have been around for a long time, and I have met with people from all walks of life. Having the opportunity to meet with people from other cultures and from different social statuses could be a learning experience for anyone. You would be surprised to discover how much you can learn from others by listening to them, speaking with them, or just observing their ways of doing things. Sometimes we think that the way we do things is the right way to do whatever it is that we are doing. Being a good listener, not being afraid of asking questions, and observing others handling certain situations could be beneficial to you. It might help you to save time and money and to be more efficient. Some people say that a smart person is the one who listens to others and asks questions. I agree.

Some of the things that I have practiced through my entire life whenever possible are listening, speaking, asking questions, and observing others going about their daily chores. Asking questions when in doubt is a smart thing to do. Those of us who do so have a better chance of being respected and are often better recognized by others than those who remain silent. Some of my friends and relatives still wonder how I was able to do so much with so little. And when I try to explain to them how I did it, in most cases they respond by saying they could never do what I did. I tell them never to say that they cannot do something that can be done without first trying. I truly believe that most of the things I have done can be done by anyone with common sense and average intelligence. I don't consider myself smarter than any average person. If I can do it, so can you.

Some people create their own obstacles and excuses when they do not want to do something they believe would take too much of their free or leisure time. They don't realize that excuses are not reasons, so they continue their journey to nowhere. While I was in college, people around me at home and at work often told me that I should give up some of my activities and enjoy life a little more. They could not understand how I kept myself so busy without even taking a vacation or spending some time with my friends. Then as time went by and they witnessed my success, several of my coworkers came to me for advice. They came to me thinking that I was smarter than they because of my success. But what they failed to remember was that while they were away somewhere having fun, I was busy doing things I thought were important to me in order to reach my goal. That is why I believe anyone can do what I did if they work hard for it; my success is not because I am smarter than they are.

The message I conveyed to my friends and coworkers years ago is the same message I want to convey to readers today. One should never be afraid or ashamed of failure. Instead, if you fail, find the reason for it without making up excuses. Things happen for a reason. And once you find the reason for your failure, do not underestimate yourself. Think positive and with conviction. Make a promise to yourself that you are going to make it regardless of what it is that you are trying to do. Evidently we are talking about something within our reach, not about something out of this planet. How I did it all might surprise you. First of all, I must bring back some lessons learned during my childhood. My parents never expected to get something for nothing; if we wanted something, we had to work for it. Sacrifices and challenges were part of our everyday life. These simple lessons learned as a child made it easier for me to face the difficult situations that I have encountered as an adult.

Those fortunate enough to have parents who loved and cared for them tend to see life from a different perspective from those whose parents failed to prepare them for today's complex society. People who believe in themselves and are not afraid to endure the challenges and sacrifices they might have to face on their road to success are those who most likely will reach their goals. Readers might say that I am repeating myself on certain issues, and they are correct. But there is a reason for it. I want the readers to remember my purpose for writing this book. I would like for them to keep in mind some of the simple things that I have mentioned throughout my book. I believe these simple things could help them to improve their quality of life. And before I go on with the next topic, I will tell readers how I did it and what it took for me to do it all.

Before you begin your journey in search of success, you must be certain that you want to do whatever it is you are about to start. You set your goal, and depending on what it is that you want to accomplish, you make a list of the things you will need to complete your project. Presenting the sequence of events in a chronological and simple way could make your project more interesting. Do not depend on anyone else to do anything for you. If it happens, fine; if not, so be it. And most importantly, be prepared to make decisions and to endure sacrifices, and perhaps disappointments. On the road to my remarkable achievements, I experienced some of the things cited above, but I never doubted my potential to reach my goal. I did it all by asking questions, following advice, observing others, and experiencing a certain degree of sacrifice—but first of all, by believing in me.

You Can Do It Too

There are people who spend a lifetime hoping and wishing for things they would like to have or to do. Some of them convince themselves that they can't do it and have an excuse for everything they claim that they can't do. This kind of behavior is difficult to explain. Unfortunately, most of these people have the potential and the ability to learn whatever it is they are claiming they cannot do. The problem is that they don't even know they have the potential to learn. This is why we hear people say that everybody needs somebody. In my case, I knew the potential and the ability to learn were there, but I was not confident that I could handle an added responsibility besides the ones I already had. Then after years of doing things without any incentive to improve my quality of life, I found my somebody. His name was Pablo, and by now readers know very well who he was.

Readers are also aware that I was an "A" student throughout all my school years. I have also mentioned that I have never considered myself smarter than any average person. I will tell you why. I believe that any person willing and determined to reach her or his goals the way I did could achieve similar results. For example, I always wanted to be an "A" student, so I worked hard for it. I made sure my schoolwork was on time and as flawless as I could make it be. I was determined to do whatever it took to reach my goals, including staying up until the late night hours to complete my schoolwork. I was always proud of my work, and I never worried about facing difficult times or having to make sacrifices. Chances are that without my conviction and my sacrifices to do well on everything I did, I wouldn't have been an "A" student. That is why I feel that anyone willing to do what I did could be an excellent student and reach his or her goals as I did.

I am convinced that if you want something, you should earn it by your own hard work. If you want to be an excellent student or whatever it is that you are searching for, study and work hard for it. It is a wonderful feeling to be able to say, "I did it." And keep in mind that most of us, if not all, need somebody to help and to guide us through the beginning of the long journey to success. I did it by asking questions when in doubt, by following the advice of reliable sources, and by never giving up when facing difficult situations. There are other things just as important that I experienced while on the road to my success. So I would like to let the readers know that if I did it, they can do it, too.

Being a Senior Citizen

Now that I have reached the special and delicate stage of my life of being a senior citizen, I will try to explain to the readers, in my opinion, what being a senior citizen is really like. I had heard people say that being old is like being a child once again. And I never gave it a thought. But now that I am reaching my eightieth birthday, I have certainly given it a thought. It seems to me that there is some truth in what people have been saying, though it might not be so for every elderly person. Considering myself as an example, when I compare the way I used to go about performing my daily activities when I was young, and the way I do them now, I have noticed a significant difference. However, based on my health condition, it is difficult to determine what is causing the changes in my performance. Let me explain what I mean.

I am a patient of a degenerative brain disease that causes negative changes in its patients, physically and mentally as well. And the fact is that not even the medical experts with advanced technology and billions of dollars in research can discover what causes this devastating disease. Although the great majority of patients are elderly, there are a number of young adults suffering from the disease. It is a matter of concern for patients and medical professionals because there are other health conditions that could cause similar changes in the body and in the brain. For example, forgetting names, dates, and places is common in the elderly with or without having a brain disease. This makes it difficult for doctors to diagnose their patients correctly. In the following chapter, I will let readers know about the devastating disease that I will endure for the rest of my life. Furthermore, this disease doesn't only affect its patients; it creates a difficult and complex situation for family members. They face a very serious decision to make. I consider myself lucky for having family members near me: Freddy, Peter Jr., his wife Sonia, and my sister Benedicta when she is not away.

Being a senior citizen is not an easy task, but it does not mean that you are through with life. Some people make their lives difficult as they get older and cannot function like when they were young. Some of them become angry and frustrated and refuse to accept certain changes happening in their bodies and in their minds. Unfortunately, this kind of behavior only makes their lives more difficult and creates stress, not only for them but also for their loved ones. They refuse to accept reality, and as a result, they seem unhappy and appear older than what they are. I consider getting old a difficult task because there is no choice; once you get old, you stay old. Furthermore, some people don't think of getting old as a dignified stage of our lives. Therefore, they seem to ignore the fact that they will become less appealing, much slower, and more dependent on help from others than when they were young. As a result, they work themselves into a sad and unhealthy life as senior citizens.

Regardless of the struggles and difficulties mentioned above, you can enjoy life as a senior citizen if you really want to. I am enjoying my life as a senior citizen even while suffering from a brain disease, and I see no reason why you can't do it as well. Besides suffering from the devastating disease and approaching eighty years of age, I am still doing the things that I have always enjoyed doing. Instead of complaining and getting angry and frustrated, I keep myself occupied and stay in touch with friends and relatives. I also travel to Texas frequently to see my grandson. I believe being a senior citizen is a special stage in our lives. It is special because it is something that can't be put on hold; you are in it for the rest of your life. So it is up to you to make the best of your life as a senior citizen for the benefit of all. And as I always say, if I can do it, so can you.

LIVING WITH PARKINSON'S DISEASE

Parkinson's is a progressive and debilitating brain disease that, eventually, will destroy the brain, causing death. There are five stages in Parkinson's disease. During its early stages, among other things, it affects the way we move, leading the patient to slow down. By the late stages, it is impossible for the patient to move without the help of others. Some Parkinson's patients show symptoms similar to those with Alzheimer's disease. Also, there have been cases when a patient has been diagnosed with Parkinson's and later on been found not to have the disease. Some early symptoms of the disease are slow thinking, memory lapses, and stooped posture. At the present time and as I write this book, I am experiencing these three symptoms.

As you read my book, you can understand the messages that I try to convey to readers through my writing, hoping they can benefit from them. I am aware of the fact that I often repeat myself. But I do it for a reason. I want to be sure that readers get the message I am trying to convey about every topic of my book. It is evident that my life did not end when I was diagnosed with Parkinson's disease. There is no definite test for Parkinson's and its cause is unknown, although the physician James Parkinson wrote a report about it in the nineteenth century.

I was diagnosed with Parkinson's disease on June 4, 2007. Since then, there have been interesting changes in my life. Regardless of the nature of these changes, I have always tried to make the best of each one of them, with great results. I am confident that if you have the disease, you can do it, too. Seven years is not a very long time, but I am certain that I had the disease for many years before I was diagnosed with it. I will explain to readers why I believe that. I do not remember the exact date, but it was approximately twenty years before the diagnosis when I experienced my right thumb often freezing. I went to a doctor at the Methodist Hospital in Brooklyn, and he gave me a cortisone shot in my finger. Then he told me that the condition would likely come back because the cortisone shot was only a temporary relief.

Years later, again, I noticed something unusual happening on my right thumb. At times it would shake, and though not too often, it would freeze in one position. As a result, I went back to the hospital to see a doctor. I went through various tests and x-rays, and did very well in all of them. The doctor told me everything seemed fine, except that the x-rays showed a tiny black spot in my brain. He said it was not an emergency, but it had to be watched.

Soon after my second visit to the hospital, I moved away from the Park Slope community and purchased a house in the Dyker Heights community, both in Brooklyn, where I am living at the present time. Therefore, I needed to find a new doctor in my new neighborhood. After a short search, I was lucky to find Doctor Wagdy Girgis, a remarkable family physician. He became my primary doctor, and we developed a friendly relationship that was, and still is, very important to me, especially when suffering from such a disease as Parkinson's. This is one of the reasons why I feel that a good relationship between doctor and patient is so important. A few years ago I felt very sick while visiting my daughter in Texas. Emmaline was extremely concerned about my condition and she called Dr. Girgis. She explained to him what was happening to me, and he told her how serious my condition was. She was told to take me immediately to the nearest hospital emergency room. And so she did. It was a kidney condition, which could have been fatal if not treated in time. I truly believe Dr. Girgis saved my life that day.

One day during a regular visit, I told Dr. Girgis about the tiny spot in my brain shown in the x-rays taken by my previous doctor. I asked him if he thought I had Parkinson's disease. He responded by saying that he needed to see the black spot in my brain before coming to any conclusion. He sent me to an imaging center for a brain MRI, and as expected, it showed the black spot. We talked about it, and he said that I should see a neurologist, who could answer my questions about Parkinson's disease. Then he advised me to see Dr. Anthony Maniscalco, so I did.

Dr. Maniscalco is a great doctor with a friendly personality. When I visited him for the first time, he listened to my story and asked me some specific questions. Then, after he tested some of my movements, he diagnosed me with Parkinson's disease. From then on, I have faithfully followed his advice, and he has always offered me his professional support, something that I need and appreciate as well. Now I knew with certainty that this health condition will be with me for the rest of my life. I considered what to do. There were a number of things I could do. But do not expect me to sit down and cry, or to believe that it was the end of my life. There was one thing I knew without a doubt: from then on, my life would never be the same.

I was not surprised with the diagnosis because that was what I expected. Dr. Maniscalco just made it official. Freddy was the first member of the family to know because he was with me. Other members of the family were not surprised because we had been talking about it for a while.

I can imagine how difficult it could be for a doctor to tell his or her patients that they have such a devastating disease. Also, the patients' reaction when they are told they have the disease could be of concern to the doctor. The fact that some Parkinson's symptoms are found in other unrelated diseases makes it more difficult for doctors to make an accurate diagnosis. It is of utmost importance for patients to tell the doctor in detail what is bothering them and what they have felt or are still feeling. Keeping information from the doctor would not help in any way, but it could make the situation more difficult for the doctor, and also for the patient.

Some people are devastated when they become aware they have the disease, and I understand why. So I will explain to readers certain things that I have learned through the years living with Parkinson's disease, hoping they can benefit from it. Parkinson's is one of the most incredible brain degenerative diseases within the medical field. Based on my own experiences and my observation of others living with the disease, I can honestly tell readers that there are many ways for them to continue their quality of life while living with the disease. Although there will be changes beyond our control in how we perform our daily activities, it is not a death sentence in any way. Some people with Parkinson's live a very long life. So it is up to us to do whatever is possible to live a normal life, instead of giving up and living in misery for the rest of our years.

When Dr. Maniscalco told me that I had the disease, obviously it was no time to celebrate. It was time for me to start my new life, officially living with Parkinson's disease. The first thing I did was to search for information about the disease. I purchased and read several books about it, attended conferences on the topic, and joined the Michael J. Fox Foundation. Though it has been almost seven years since my diagnosis, I have been able to continue my daily activities as usual. Rather than saying *why me*, I informed my relatives and friends about my condition. Because Parkinson's is such a devastating disease and it will be with you for the rest of your life, it is important to talk about it with your friends and loved ones. It is the right thing to do for the benefit of all. The support from family and friends is essential. Knowing that you are not alone will give you strength, not only to cope with the disease, but to face the struggles that come along with it. As I mentioned above, I hope readers who have the disease will do what I did—get involved and learn all that they possibly can about the disease.

Remember, if you are diagnosed with Parkinson's disease, the more you learn about this horrible brain-destroyer, the better prepared you will be to make it easier for you to live with the disease. Believe me, it works. Ironically, Parkinson's, besides being a fearsome disease, is also quite interesting. As devastating as it is, the disease is hardly mentioned or discussed by anyone but researchers and patients. I say it is interesting because of the way in which the disease develops and onsets in its patients. To date, though research and studies have been conducted for almost two hundred years, the disease still remains a mystery. From the year 1817, when it was mentioned publicly for the first time, no one can tell yet what causes the disease or the reasons for the variety of ways in which it occurs in patients.

Living with Parkinson's disease can create fear and despair for anyone afflicted by it. However, it does not have to be that way. It will be that way only if you let it be so. Getting angry and complaining is not going to help anyone. It could make the situation more difficult. Patients should get well-informed about the disease. It would help them understand their condition and be aware and prepared for whatever the future will bring for them. It will be to the patients' advantage to learn as much as they can about the disease. That is what I have been doing since I was diagnosed with it. It has helped me cope with the disease and made it less painful for my loved ones to accept my condition.

I hope readers can benefit with the information that I have been providing them about this brain-wrecking disease. I could continue writing about this chronic brain disorder endlessly, but this topic was not the reason why I wrote this book. Once again I want to remind readers that when facing a situation beyond their control, do not dwell on the impossible: accept it, and move on, even if it means living with Parkinson's. Get involved, stay active, and do not be afraid or ashamed of having the disease. It was not your fault. Sometimes nature does not give us a choice.

Before I set my pen to rest, or better yet, before I give my two fingers a break, I would like to thank readers for reading my book, but most of all, I hope they learned something from it to help them improve their quality of life. To parents with young children, I would like to remind them to do their best to teach their children well; the results will be rewarding. Also, remember to tell your precious little ones every day that you love them.

Emma's Tips for a Better Life

1. Do something that could make you feel good about yourself. Help someone in need.
2. Do something that shows you care. Send a get-well card to someone who is ill.
3. When experiencing a bad situation, do not say, "Why me?" It might indicate selfishness on your part.
4. Never promise something that you cannot deliver. You might lose your credibility.
5. Do not be ashamed to ask questions. Others do it, and no one knows everything.
6. Do not challenge the impossible or issues beyond your control. You might be wasting your time and that of others.
7. Respect other people's opinions. It could incite others to respect yours.
8. Listen to the advice of others. It could prevent you from repeating mistakes you made in the past.
9. Do not try to impress anyone; just be yourself. People will appreciate you more.
10. Try to make friends, rather than enemies. You might sleep better at night.
11. Learn from your mistakes. It is the right thing to do, and their effect could be less painful.
12. Do not try to hide the obvious. You will just be kidding yourself.
13. Do not seek revenge. Seek peace instead.

14. Do not dwell on bad experiences. Try to relive good ones.
15. Do not try to hide guilt. It might be written all across your face.
16. Try to look at the positive side of things. It could make the situation less complicated and the results easier to accept.
17. Do not expect payback when doing a favor to someone. It is unethical, and it might no longer be a favor.
18. Do not remind a person of a favor done in the past. It might indicate that you are expecting something in return.
19. Do not rush to judgment without first learning the facts. You might not know what you are talking about.
20. When explaining an issue, do not make up excuses. You will look like a fool when the facts come out.

Epilogue

When I started to write this book, I had doubts about being able to do it well enough to inspire people to read it. Questions went through my mind like the wind in a storm. Where should I begin? Whom could I go to for guidance? I knew the message that I wanted to covey to readers, but so much material to tell from so many years back made me wonder if I was going to make it. I was not sure If I could put it all together in a way readers could understand my message and learn from it. I thought about it until I convinced myself that I could do it. My friends and relatives always knew that I could do it.

I thought about Pablo and Barbara and their trust in me. Although they are no longer with me, their wisdom and inspiration are. I also thought about Professor Kelber, who used to tell me that I was a courageous woman. The last time we spoke about my book project, he told me to write one page a day, and before I knew it, I would have my book. The memories of these three incomparable human beings inspired me to write my book.

While speaking about wisdom and inspirations, I will tell you something that could give you food for thought. While in Texas for my grandson Gavin's sixth birthday, I noticed he was wearing a shirt with the letters "LSU" on the front. So I asked him if he was planning on going to college. Here is what he said: "Yes, Nana, I am going to college, and I don't care what people say;

even if I am sick, I am going to college, and nobody can stop me because I am going to college, Nana."

His response left me momentarily breathless. Then I asked him if Daddy had said that to him. He responded by saying, "No, Nana, it's me; nobody told me to say it. It's me." Not only what he said took me by surprise, but also the convincing way in which he said it.

Another time, when he was five years old, we were playing with rockets, and I asked him if he wanted to be an astronaut. He said, "No, Nana, I am going to be a doctor." I asked him why, and he said, "Because I want to make people feel better." Unlike other children his age, Gavin is a pleasure to be with and welcome every place he goes. And the credit for all this goes to his parents.

I ask parents to prepare their children to enter our permissive society with a set goal for their future. Parents should not wait for the child to begin his or her education by following just what our society has to offer. Sadly, in today's world, anything goes. Keep in mind that no child of any race or religion is born knowing anything. Evidently it is the parents' responsibility to start feeding that empty brain with the right things. This is exactly what Gavin's parents did, and the results are obvious. If this does not happen, the child will be vulnerable to follow the wrong direction instead of enjoying a productive future.

It is evident that Gavin's parents have been teaching him well, and it has worked. Gavin's mention of Louisiana State University (LSU) indicates that they have been talking to him about college, for his father is an LSU graduate. Once again I bring back my conviction about childhood. Emmaline and Aaron are doing for Gavin what my parents did for me. I also mentioned earlier that lessons learned during my childhood were applied to my children. Now my daughter and her husband are doing for their child what I did for her. This is an indication of the importance of childhood in a child's development. Parents must play their role in their children's early development for the benefit of all.

As I approach the completion of my book, I want readers to know that I tried my best to comply with my purpose for writing it. I have also tried to be truthful to the best of my recollection in all that I have written. My opinions and comments throughout the entire book are my own. At no point in my writing did I portray myself as being perfect or above anyone. I have made mistakes and bad decisions. I am simply human. I can honestly say that I always have a reason for my actions. I understand why, during the course of our lives, there are moments in which we make a decision or take an action against our norm or our belief, almost always for the sake of something or someone.

All of the above being said, I want to remind readers, especially minority women, to believe in themselves and not to be afraid to express their feelings or to ask questions when in doubt. Keep in mind that no one is perfect and nobody knows everything. Now that you have read my life story, I hope it makes a difference in your quality of life, that being my primary reason for writing this book. I also hope you enjoyed reading it as much as I enjoyed writing it.

ABOUT THE AUTHOR

Emma Gomez grew up on a farm in the mountains of Puerto Rico and moved to New York City in 1953 after completing high school. She faced challenges at a time when minority women were taken for granted. This book is a testament to her struggle and endurance. In plain and simple language, she shares with readers how she overcame obstacles and achieved her success and goals. I have known Emma my entire life. She is a strong, independent, and courageous woman. I have been fortunate to know Emma and have her influence my life. My name is Samantha and I am Emmaline's friend and her class-mate for almost all our school years. We also share our birthday on the same date.

Why I Wrote This Book

My primary reason for writing this book was my desire to share my life story and experiences with readers, especially minority women. Being a minority woman myself, I hope to help readers find ways to improve their quality of life. Although this book was written primarily for women, it can benefit men as well. There are men who sometimes hurt the ones they love, creating a negative environment with serious consequences. As conflicts develop, they become aware of their actions, thinking in hindsight, *If I had known better.* I believe my life story could be of interest to readers from all walks of life. It is a story of challenges, success, and most importantly, how I reached my goals.

Readers will understand why I concentrate on women more than men. In plain and simple language, I bring to readers' attention some factors that, although part of everyday life, are often overlooked or taken for granted. It would give me great satisfaction if, after reading this book, readers say they learned something from it. I hope they use my experiences as learning tools to help them understand that success doesn't come easily; it involves a certain degree of sacrifice. My experiences are a clear example of dedication, endurance, and sacrifice. These topics are fully explained in my book. I would like readers to feel as if they were talking to me rather than reading a book.

Comments about My Book

"True grit"—that's exactly what you get when you read this exciting true story of this self-made woman, Emma Gomez. Within the short time that I have known her, she has unselfishly given of herself to all without prejudice, seeking to give rather than to receive. And that's the point of the story you are about to read. Now she gives to you, the readers, just as she has given to all who have crossed her path. Enjoy the ride.

—James G. Nolan Jr.

Emma is a woman of integrity and resolve who has reached remarkable success through her lifelong struggles and sacrifices. She hopes that by reading her book, readers learn something from it that could help them to improve their quality of life. Her book is inspiring and worth reading. Emma is the best mother of all times, and I am proud to be her son.

—Peter Gomez Jr.

Ms. Emma is a good woman. She helps me with my homework and picks me up from school when my mom cannot do it. Every time I get 95 percent or higher in my schoolwork, she gives me something. I like to read her book.

—Alan Rojas (eight years old)

I am certain that everyone who reads this book will love it and will learn something from it. Emma's writing style is unique: like talking rather than reading. Her book is well written and easy to read.

—Benedicta Rodriguez